MW01010380

TABLE OF CONTENTS

DEDICATION — **Pg. 4**

ACKNOWLEDGEMENTS — **Pg. 5**

FORWARD – KIDS CAN! — **Pg. 6**

CHAPTER 1 – KIDS CAN BE! — **Pg. 8**

CHAPTER 2 – KIDS CAN HEAR! — **Pg. 23**

CHAPTER 3 – KIDS CAN DO! — **Pg. 40**

CHAPTER 4 – KIDS CAN GO! — **Pg. 51**

CHAPTER 5 – KIDS CAN SPEAK! — **Pg. 65**

CHAPTER 6 – GROWNUPS CAN! — **Pg. 79**

MINISTRY PHOTOS — **Pg. 84**

RESOURCES — **Pg. 98**

**All Scripture references are English Standard Version unless otherwise marked.

DEDICATION:

This book is dedicated to all children everywhere. God desires to have communion with, fill, anoint, equip and send out these little prayer warriors with strength, wisdom, sharpness, authority and power to do mighty exploits for Him.

That we would only be wise enough to learn from them.

ACKNOWLEDGEMENTS

Thank you, Allen, for being my husband, my friend, my love for the last 30 some years. Thank you for being the tether that holds me to the ground here on Earth!

Thank you, Sarah and Raychael, for being the best daughters a mom could ever ask for! You've made my life fuller and more interesting as you grew – you are why I wrote this book!

Thank you to my great family at Hunters Point Celebration Center in Lebanon, TN. There I have found depth and new growth. I've found God's voice and the peace that passes all understanding. I've found new friends that I hope to make old ones out of – bless you all for your part in encouraging me and standing with me.

Thanks to Pastors Marc and Susan Huddleston at HPCC. Your integrity and desire to hear God's leading and voice above all is incredible, and I love watching you both worship! Thanks, Susan, for all the editing and insight. You are a treasure trove of wisdom from the Lord.

Special thanks go to Caron, who worked so hard trying to kill my many punctuation errors – you are so patient, my friend, and, many, many, thanks! Too many commas?

To my artists, Daniel and Josh, you have doubled my joy with your talents and hard work. I love you guys, and am so very proud of you both!

Thank you, Sarah, for being my old "war buddy" in the trenches when we were first learning about this incredible process! I love you so much! We did some pretty strange stuff, cool stuff, scary stuff, fun stuff and deep stuff. I look forward to the future where I can continue to learn from you! Why can't we........

Thank you, Jeanette, for being there and encouraging me throughout this entire process. You are a friend that is closer than a sister, and you've kept me plenty of times from myself. I love you!

To those who've encouraged, guided, allowed, empowered, equipped and been a friend, you all are a part of this book – extra feather pillow for you all in Heaven!

To the kids and parents who've walked with us on this journey – I can't say how proud I am of all of you and your willingness to "go for God", especially when we were learning ourselves! I love and honor your walk with Him!

More than everyone listed above, this book and my heart belong to Jesus. He's my life, my breath, my all in all, and if I didn't have Him, this book would not have been written. He's given me His heart for His children and a vision for their future. I love you, Abba!

FORWARD

Children are so cool! They have their own special persona that gives spark and buoyancy to everyday life. Seeing things through their eyes keeps God's wonders before me, and things are always new and fresh. It is amazing to me how God loves to connect with these little ones so lovingly and gently. He is a good Daddy!

I never tire of watching children fall in love with Jesus. It is awesome to see the looks on their faces during prayer when Jesus whispers secrets to their waiting ears. I am always thrilled at the joy and excitement that comes when they share their messages with me from their special Friend.

I remember the first time I was introduced to the concept of kids in ministry. The children's pastor at our church, Sarah Turner, and I were going to Georgia to a conference on children in 1998. Up to that point, I was unaware what God was really up to with the kids we ministered to. We knew that something was going on with the children in our church because God was leading us to do things we had never done, and we were seeing incredible results. Sarah and I just thought we were the only ones this was happening to, and we didn't really understand it.

Imagine our surprise when we walked into a huge auditorium with a thousand adults and kids! Sarah and I looked at each other and wondered what kind of chaos this was going to be, but we were so wrong! We came to the understanding right then that we were NOT the only ones being led by God into a new direction of children's ministry. The speakers were outstanding, and the idea that kids could do ministry effectively was intriguing, but was it really possible?

We got our answer at the end of the first evening. The last speaker invited people down to the front to get prayer for strength and vision in their ministries. I expected the adult ministry team to meet us at the front, but instead, a whole line of kids, ages 6-14, met us. Sarah and I stood side by side as several little girls came up to pray for us. Immediately upon laying their hands on us, we were both ignited with electricity that I had never felt before. Constant waves of this power ran through us as we lay on the floor while children powerfully prayed for us. We laid there for over an hour, just absorbing what God was doing. God had spoken, and we were in for the trip of a lifetime.

I am not an expert on children; I am a very simple person. You don't need big words or have to be a rocket scientist to hear from God and to teach children to do the same. Jesus makes it so easy and uncomplicated, and I like it that way! I encourage you, as you read this book to see children through Jesus' eyes. Listen and learn from Him, and I think you will find that YOU will grow deeper in relationship with Jesus as you bring your children closer to Him.

In this book, you will find some thoughts, tips, and testimonies regarding children and their ability to understand and act on the voice of God. Enjoy the journey. I pray God will fill you and your kids to overflowing, and then some! Read, learn, then go out and teach them to "do the stuff" because "Kids Can"!

Karen Barnes

KIDS CAN BE!

When children are taught and trained that they are His, and that they have power from on high, amazing things can happen. God has proven over and over that the adults are not the only ones who can be anointed and move freely in the Spirit. More and more, we are observing children around the world who move in power and hear God's words for themselves.

First, though, they need to know their rightful place in the Kingdom of God, and there is no "too early" age. As we begin teaching our children what their rights are, who they are called to be, and how they may access those rights, we will see more kids become acclimated to a deeper life in Jesus. They will exhibit more maturity, see and hear with more clarity, have incredible trust, and stand with an unwavering faith that will move mountains.

Where do children fit into God's Kingdom? In the same place as you and I do – side by side with Jesus. Once kids know who they are in Christ, and begin to put that into practice, everything is as open to them as it is to us. As we explain principles in their terminology, pray for their hearts and minds to be open, project the attitude of "yes, you can get this" rather than, "oh, you are just too young for this", then we see growth, understanding, positive expectation, and finally, application.

Kids love stories, and I like to act out Bible stories for them during my teaching times. I am an animated person, so it is not hard for me to keep their attention. I try to use "today's terminology" as I act out the stories. This makes everything more real for them, and causes them to better understand the message and concepts. To explain the concept of destiny, for instance, I may tell them a story of God talking to them before they were born, and telling them His plan for their lives. (Jeremiah 29:11"For I know the plans I have for you, declares the LORD, plans for welfare and not for evil, to give you a future and a hope.")

Jeremiah 1:5 says, "Before I formed you in the womb, I knew you, and before you were born, I consecrated you". I believe God knew us totally before birth. He created us, so as He fashioned us, He spoke words of destiny over us and looked at what we were designed and set apart (consecrated) to do. David spoke these words regarding his relationship with God before birth, "Upon You I have leaned from before my birth; You are He who took me from my mother's womb. My praise is continually of You" Psalm 71:6.

I tell the children that God had it all figured out what they would become and what they would do for Him. After they were born, however, they become so busy with the things of this new life, like learning to crawl, eat, talk, and walk, that they easily forget what God told them about His plan for them. One day, however, they begin to hear a voice calling their name, and they start to feel like they want to be a teacher, or an engineer, or a doctor. That voice is God reminding them of what the plan is for their lives, causing them to feel a call toward that plan. That is what "destiny" is, and everyone has that. Teaching children in this way makes sense to them, and it makes them eager to be able to hear God's voice for direction. It is so awesome to watch them diligently listen for God's voice to be "reminded" what their "destiny" is!

God can certainly lead and speak to children; David was a great example. In Psalm 71:5, David blesses God and says, "For you, O Lord, are my hope, my trust, O LORD, from my youth"; and again in Psalm 71:17, "O God, from my youth you have taught me, and I still proclaim your wondrous deeds". What a great thing it is to be taught by God Himself in your youth! Children need to be taught, with great assurance, that God WILL teach them, lead them, and speak to them!

The first thing children need to realize in their youth is that they need a Savior just as adults do. They must realize their sin and that God paid the price for that sin through the sacrifice, death, and resurrection of Jesus. Recently, I was teaching at a summer kid's camp that my 8 year old grandson was attending. One evening, we presented the plan of salvation to the children. I remember explaining to them, through acting out a scene, how we are separated from God and only Jesus can bring us back to God where we can hear His voice, feel His presence, and be led by Him with joy.

My grandson attends an awesome church where the children's pastor is tremendous at explaining and teaching concepts, but, this particular night, I saw his little eyes change as this hit home to him. The more I spoke, the deeper the knowledge of his own sin was becoming to him. It was apparent by the look on his face that he was "getting it"; God was speaking directly to him. I gave an invitation for salvation, and he was one of many that responded by asking Jesus to come in, clean up his sin, and help him live for Christ all his days.

Although he had probably heard that many times in his church, there was that moment when he and God had an appointed time to meet, and the cloud for him was lifted. Each child will respond to Jesus at different times and in different situations. God's timing is best. Continually putting the message out there to them is vitally important. This is, of course, the foundation for everything else they learn, do, experience, and live out for the rest of their lives.

Part of growing in our Christian life is to understand that, once we ask Jesus in, we become HIS, and we are not our own anymore. Children need to know that they are now royalty! Revelation 1:6 says, "And hath made us kings and priests unto God and His Father; to Him be glory and dominion for ever and ever. Amen" (KJV). 1Peter 2:9 also talks about this when it says, "But ye are a chosen race, a royal priesthood, a holy nation, a people for His own possession, that you may proclaim the excellencies of Him who called you out of darkness into his marvelous light." Romans 8:14 tell us, "For all who are led by the Spirit of God, are sons of God." We belong to God, and that makes us sons and daughters, which means we have an inheritance. Just as children of an earthly king have rights and privileges, so do we AND our children.

We are flesh and blood, but we are also spirit and soul. We were born on this earth, but our eternal inheritance, our REAL "life" is in the Spirit. We are a spirit inside a body, not the other way around. The spiritual realm is much more real than the natural. We are only here for a short time before we go on to another reality, the spiritual realm, for eternity. Which realm we go to, heaven or hell, depends on whether or not we decide to turn our lives over to God and allow Him to walk through us.

As Christians, God becomes our Father in the spiritual realm when we turn over complete control of our lives to Him. We are tied to God and are His children. Romans 8:16-17 states "The Spirit Himself bears witness with our spirit that <u>we are children of God</u>, and if children, then <u>heirs</u> – heirs of God and fellow heirs with Christ, provided we suffer with Him in order that we may also be glorified with Him." We have rights in the spiritual realm just as we do in the physical one. We actually have dual citizenship in BOTH realms! We have one foot on one side and one foot on the other. God intended this for us so that we can experience both and have authority in both. Ephesians 2:19 says, "So then you are no longer strangers and aliens, but you are fellow citizens with the saints and members of the household of God." Philippians 3:20 also declares, "But our citizenship is in heaven, and from it we await a Savior, the Lord Jesus Christ."

This opens up a much bigger world to us AND our children! The son of a king does not have to wait until he is "of age" to enjoy the benefits, privileges, and authority of being the king's son. He automatically receives those things upon his birth. The good news is this: so do we and our kids! Therefore, we receive those benefits in two realms – here on earth and in the heavenly realm. Once our kids begin to see this at an early age, and we reinforce this every chance we get, it gives them confidence. Their outlook on life becomes totally different, and they understand their position and authority. They can take more ground, comprehend deeper things of the Spirit, and walk in the manifest presence of God on a daily basis.

The Holy Spirit also helps us to learn more about our position. Joel 2:28 says, "And it shall come to pass afterward, that I will pour out my Spirit on all flesh; your sons and your daughters shall prophesy, your old men shall dream dreams, and your young men shall see visions." Notice that it says on ALL flesh – there are no restrictions given. He even goes on to expressly define certain age groups –"your <u>sons</u> and your <u>daughters</u>; your <u>old</u> men; your <u>young</u> men".

Once children realize who they are in Christ, they need to learn how to receive from the Lord in different ways. Just as we have our natural senses, we also have spiritual senses. God communicates to us through these senses. Consider the following:

Psalm 119:18 "Open my eyes, that I may behold wondrous things out of your law."

Ephesians 1:17-18 "That the God of our Lord Jesus Christ, the Father of glory, may give unto you a spirit of wisdom and revelation in the knowledge of him; having the eyes of your heart enlightened, that ye may know what is the hope to which He has called you, what are the riches of His glorious inheritance in the saints,"

Matthew 13:16 "But blessed are your eyes, for they see, and your ears, for they hear."

John 10:27 "My sheep hear my voice, and I know them, and they follow me."

Psalm 34:8 "Oh, taste and see that the LORD is good! Blessed is the man who takes refuge in him!"

Psalm 119:103 "How sweet are your words to my taste, sweeter than honey to my mouth!"

Luke 14:24 "for I tell you, none of those men who were invited shall taste my banquet.'"

2Corinthians 2:15-16 "For we are the aroma of Christ to God among those who are being saved and among those who are perishing, to one a fragrance from death to death, to the other a fragrance from life to life. Who is sufficient for these things?"

Act 17:27 "That they should seek God, in the hope that they might feel their way toward him and find him. Yet he is actually not far from each one of us..."

We, as well as our children, can experience God in the fullest ways possible by using all the spiritual senses He's given to us. We have that right as children of the King, with citizenship in both realms. Through seeing His glory, hearing His words, enjoying the fragrance of His presence, tasting the goodness of the Lord, and sensing His loving touch, children can be drawn into a more intimate encounter with God.

We must overcome the mindset we have had for centuries that kids are of little concern to God and they must be silent in all things. Scripture says quite the opposite about them. I Timothy 4:12 says, "Let no one look down on your youthfulness, but rather, in speech, conduct, love, faith and purity, show yourselves an example of those who believe" (NASB). I don't believe Paul was only speaking to young Timothy at this time. I believe that verse encourages children that their youth is not a negative factor or consequence, then goes on to empower them to actually BE the example to others by telling them exactly how to do so.

Jeremiah gives us another example of God's belief in and empowerment of young people in Jeremiah 1:6-7. "Then I said, "Ah, Lord GOD! Behold, I do not know how to speak, for I am only a youth." But the LORD said to me, "Do not say, 'I am only a youth'; for to all to whom I send you, you shall go, and whatever I command you, you shall speak."

There will be times when our kids will waver – who among us has NOT wavered? As in any other time of learning and growing, there are days when we grow weak, or days when we doubt ourselves and the God who loves us. There will be times that children will wonder if they really are called of God, if God really can use them, speak to them, and fill them. What does God say about that?

2 Corinthians 12:9-10 declares, "But He said to me, My grace is sufficient for you, for My power is made perfect in weakness. Therefore I will boast all the more gladly of my weaknesses, so that the power of Christ may rest upon me. For the sake of Christ, then, I am content with weaknesses, insults, hardships, persecutions, and calamities. For when I am weak, then I am strong."

1Corinthians 1:27 states, "But God hath chosen the foolish things of the world to confound the wise; and God hath chosen the weak things of the world to confound the things which are mighty" (KJV).

People usually see children as foolish and weak. God sees them as empowered, equals, strong, wise, insightful, mature - a force to be reckoned with - when they are listening and obedient to Him.

Most things in life start out small. They grow, mature, and then reach complete growth, producing fruit. It is the same for children. Yes, they start out in immaturity, having to be taught everything. We have all had to go down that same road. If we believe in the children, however, training them from the start, allowing them to walk beside us instead of behind us, and giving them what they need to grow, then they can become mature more quickly. Hebrews 5:14 says, "But solid food is for the mature, who because of practice have their senses trained to discern good and evil" (NASB). Our job as parents and leaders is to assist in their training!

We want our kids to stretch out and do things that will encourage them and help them mature, but we also want to be sure to use appropriate guided caution and prayer. Children are similar to tomato plants. When the plants are placed in the ground in the spring, they are small and subject to the weather. All care is taken to watch the skies, and if a storm arises, the plants are covered to protect them, until the storm has passed. We should do the same with our kids. Be watchful, but cover them as needed during heavy storms, but allow them to "stay in the garden" even through occasional rains, which really are good for them.

With young tomato plants, it is necessary to tie them to a stake to keep them growing strong and straight. Once that stem has grown to a certain diameter or height, it is necessary to loosen the ties a bit, and it is sometimes best to place the strings in a different position, in order to facilitate their growth. Again, kids are the same. Children need some guidance - a little direction as to which way to go. Then, as they grow stronger, we need to "let go" a little more and a little more to accommodate the growth which God is causing in their lives.

Earlier, we discussed the fact that God is NOT a respecter of persons. (Acts 10:34). "And Peter opened his mouth and said, Of a truth I perceive that God is no respecter of persons" (ASV). Peter did not go on to say, "except for children". Kids are included in that statement. Why would God NOT want to speak to children?

Knowing that God is not a respecter of persons, knowing that children CAN hear from and be used by God, knowing that children receive the same thing as adults receive in salvation, and knowing that children are therefore equal to adults in God's eyes and in the Kingdom, puts a whole new perspective on the Word of God. We must read it with open eyes to these facts. The Bible looks a little different when we see its direction, commands, and promises are for CHILDREN as well as adults!

Look at these verses in this new light, and consider how they apply to not only adults, but to kids as well:

*Acts 1:8 "But you will receive power, when the Holy Spirit has come upon you, and you will be My witnesses in Jerusalem and in all Judea and in Samaria, and to the end of the earth."

*Matthew 10:1 "And He called to Him His twelve disciples and gave them authority over unclean spirits, to cast them out, and to heal every disease and every affliction."

*Luke 10:19 "Behold, I have given you authority to tread on serpents and scorpions, and over all the power of the enemy, and nothing shall hurt you."

These are all things kids are supposed to do – things they were created to do. We are all supposed to minister to each other with power and see great things happen. That is because, originally, we were designed to be in close connection with God, and power flows out from Him. We are to be without fear, without doubt, have a pure faith, and be innocent of evil. That is how God can use us all. That is the example the kids give us. That is why they can do the things they do. No doubt, fearless, innocent – that is the way it is supposed to be!

Now consider these Scriptures with the fresh awareness that they apply just as much to children as they do to adults.

*Romans 8:11 "But if the Spirit of the Him who raised Jesus from the dead dwells in you, He who raised Christ Jesus from the dead will also give life to your mortal bodies through His Spirit who dwells in you."

*Galatians 2:20 "I have been crucified with Christ. It is no longer I who live, but Christ who lives in me. And the life I now live in the flesh I live by faith in the Son of God, who loved me and gave himself for me."

*I Corinthians 6: 19-20 "Or do you not know that your body is a temple of the Holy Spirit within you, whom you have from God? You are not your own, for you were bought with a price. So glorify God in your body."

Many times I have heard comments from children such as, "I can't do that" or "I'm too little". I always remind them of 1Corinthians 3:16 which says, "Do you not know that you are God's temple and that God's Spirit dwells in you?" God lives within THEM! If He lives there, resides there, is constantly there, what does that mean for them, I ask? What kind of power do they have? What could their hands do? What could their feet or their arms do? What could they say or see? Had they ever thought that Jesus could see someone through their eyes?

It is not just this current generation that has experienced mighty moves of God on children. He has moved on children throughout history - changing, empowering, imparting wisdom and revelation to them with each passing year. We can glimpse a sample of these awesome waves of God on kids through the journals that were written by some of the mighty men of God from past generations.

The following accounts are excerpts from David Walters book, <u>Children Aflame</u>. In the book, Walters follows men such as John Wesley, George Whitfield, D.L. Moody, and others, by recounting tales and facts from their ministries regarding children and revival in years past. Interspersed with the journal writings are Walters recollections from his own experiences with children around the world which describe how God affected their lives and situations during his ministry.

The writings are listed by date (day, month and year) with the author's name following the excerpt. Only slight changes have been made in grammar, thereby preserving them just as they were written in the original journals. Be prepared to be amazed at what God has done with children throughout the years!

16/9/1770. KINGSWOOD SCHOOL. ...29TH SAT. I was awaked between four and five, by the children vehemently crying to God. The maids went to them at five. And first one of the boys, then another, then one and another of the maids, earnestly poured out their souls before God, both for themselves and for the rest. They continued weeping and praying till nine o'clock, not thinking about meat or drink, nay, Richard Piercy took no food all the day, but remained in words or groans calling upon God. About one o'clock all the maids and three of the boys went upstairs and began praying again; and now they found the Lord's hand was not shortened; between two and three, many rejoiced with joy unspeakable. They all continued together till after four, praising the God of their salvation; indeed they seemed to have forgotten all things here below, and to think of nothing but God and heaven... John Wesley

> There have been many occasions when we have observed children of all ages, from three years to teenagers, come under the power of the Holy Spirit. Some of them have been on the floor for hours in various degrees of experiences from speaking in tongues, crying, laughing, trembling, and shaking with hands extended in worship. Surely, only the Holy Spirit can keep a child's hands raised up toward heaven for one or two hours. Often their faces have lit up with a heavenly glow. Some of the very small children have drawn pictures of heaven and angels to show their teachers what they saw during those experiences. Parents at later times testified of the changes wrought in their children's behavior after being touched by God. — DAVID WALTERS

12/5/1782. (SUNDAY) About eight I preached at Misterton; about one at Overthorpe. Many of the Epworth children were there, and their spirit spread to all around them; but the huge congregation was in the Market-place at Epworth, and the Lord, in the midst of them. The love-feast which followed, exceeded all. I never knew such a one here before. As soon as one had done speaking, another began. Several of them were children but they spoke with the wisdom of the aged, though with the fire of youth. So out of the mouth of babes and suckling's did God perfect praise... John Wesley

Some time ago I was in Vancouver, Canada. I was invited to speak at a Christian School. There were about one hundred and thirty students from ages six through eighteen that gathered together for the assembly. After some mild praise and worship I was invited to address them. I preached on "If anyone desires to come after me...." (Matt. 16:24) and encouraged them to be totally sold out for Christ. There were also about forty Asian students at the assembly who were not saved. At the end of the message I made an appeal for anyone who desired to receive Christ as their Saviour, but with no response. The Asians did not budge. I then exhorted the professing Christians to rededicate their lives to the Lord and a large crowd came forward from every age group. I prayed for the students and asked God to touch them in a special way. I then sat down with the principal and waited for the Holy Spirit to move.

After about ten minutes the Lord moved on a fifteen-year old girl. She began to pray against the demonic strongholds over the children, their school, and their homes. She then went up to a teenage boy of about sixteen, and laid hands on him and began to pray. Suddenly he fell to the ground and received a mighty deliverance. He then rose up, filled with the Holy Spirit and began to go and pray and minister to the Asian students. Within a short time they received deliverance, salvation, and the fullness of the Holy Spirit. The flame began to spread and within a short time all the children from 1st grade through 12th grade were in circles praying for each other. Many were crying out to God. Teachers came in to watch and began to weep as they saw God move upon the children. This went on for about two hours and almost every student was affected. Suddenly, some of the students began singing praises to God with great passion, raising their hands and falling on their knees. After a time, one of them stood up and said, "Let us march around the school and take it for Jesus!" The principal told me that the fifteen-year-old girl whom God had used was slightly retarded and was regarded by the students as being socially unacceptable. "But God has chosen the foolish things of the world to put to shame the wise..." (1 Corinthians 1:27). —DAVID WALTERS

8/6/1784. I CAME TO STOCKTON-ON-TEES. Here I found an uncommon work of God among the children. Many of them from six to fourteen years, were under serious impressions, and earnestly desirous to save their souls. There were upwards of sixty who constantly came to be examined and appeared to be greatly awakened. I preached at noon on, "The Kingdom of heaven is at hand"; and the people seemed to feel every word, one of whom and another sunk down upon their knees, until they were all kneeling; so I kneeled down myself, and began praying for them. Abundance of people ran back into the house. The fire kindled and ran from heart to heart, till few, if any, were unaffected. Is not this a new thing in the earth? God begins His work in children. Thus it has also been in Cornwall, Manchester, and Epworth. Thus the flame spreads to those of riper years; till at length they all know Him, and praise Him, from the least unto the greatest... John Wesley

Some years ago my wife Kathie and I were ministering to teens at a family camp outside Columbus, Ohio. Many of the teenagers were rebellious toward the things of God. We felt to minister one time to the younger children. We gathered the 5–11 year olds after supper and prayed for them for the anointing. There were approximately 30 children present. After I had prayed I sat down and waited for God to touch them. They stood around in silence. After about 10 minutes the Holy Spirit came strongly upon a little girl of about six years old. She fell to her knees and began to weep. Then one by one, other children also fell to their knees and began to weep. After a while they stood up with hands raised and began to sing in the Spirit and worship the Lord, tears still coursing down their cheeks. A little while later they bowed down again and placed their hands and foreheads on the floor, still worshipping and then praying and interceding. Intermittently, they stood and then bowed down. Some began to speak in other tongues, prophesy and have visions. One small boy of eight years had a detailed prophetic vision of the U.S.

The chapel bell rang for the evening family service. The chapel was at the top of a hill and the children began to climb up, holding on to each other, as many were still under the influence of the Spirit. Halfway up the hill, the children caught up with the reluctant teenagers, who were dragging their feet to the meeting. As the children came alongside the teens, the power of God fell upon them. They in turn fell to their knees and began to cry out to God. The smaller children laid hands on them and prayed and the teenagers were delivered from their rebellion and bondage and received the Baptism of the Holy Spirit.

The guest speaker was preparing his message and the musicians were practicing their songs. When all of the young people entered into the chapel, the Spirit of God fell powerfully upon the whole place. Many adults simply fell off their seats and received physical healings and the infilling of the Holy Spirit. That night the speaker was unable to preach his message and the musicians never sang their prepared songs. God just took over. As in John Wesley's meeting on Stockton-on-Tess, God began His work in the children.

On another occasion my wife and I were ministering at an Easter retreat held at a Christian guest house on the Isle of Wight, a small island off the south coast of England. The week-end was coming to a close, signifying the ending of the retreat. On the Sunday evening we had met for praise and ministry in the chapel, attached to the guest-house. When the meeting finished the adults and children went into the house for refreshments. The teenagers were left in the chapel still standing in a circle and singing praise songs to the Lord. After about 30 minutes a teenager came running in shouting, "David! David! Come quickly!" I went back into the chapel. A strange sight met my eyes as I entered. In the middle of the room was a young lad of about sixteen who had received salvation earlier that day. He was surrounded by a circle of teenagers. He was kneeling with his right arm and index finger extended and appeared to be in a trance. He slowly pointed around the room to each one of the teens. As he did, the power of God fell, and they dropped to the ground. The teens on the floor began to groan and cry out. Some tried to leave the room before the boy turned and pointed in their direction; but they were unable to move, as if their feet were glued. All of the teens received a wonderful deliverance and experience of God's presence. As the power of God lifted I returned to the house. Suddenly, as we were talking about the things that had happened in the chapel, the power of God came into the room and fell upon the adults and they also dropped to the floor. Some laughed, some cried, some were healed and set free.

As the Holy Spirit lifted we heard a commotion from upstairs and many of the children came running down. Some were crying and weeping, others laughing. The Holy Spirit had not left them out just because they were asleep. He had awakened them and touched them also with His mercy and grace. Man may neglect and consider children of little spiritual value, but, "...there is no partiality with God." (See Romans 2:11.) They are of great important to Him. — DAVID WALTERS

In 1741 the famous evangelist, George Whitfield, visited Edinburgh in Scotland where he preached to the boys of Herriot's Hospital. It was called a hospital because both teachers and pupils ate, slept and lived there, the boys receiving both their education and their maintenance free.

In November one of the masters told a friend about 'the remarkable behavior of his boys,' some 'who were ringleaders to the rest in vices are now spending their time reading the Bible, and books like.' At bed-time, which was 8.00 pm, they were supposed to pray, but while one said the Lord's Prayer the others used to laugh or have a carryon. 'But now, in a calm evening, through every corner of that large house, you may hear little societies worshipping the God and Father of our Lord Jesus Christ, breathing from their souls a warm and holy devotion, till late at night.'

Whitfield returned to Edinburgh in 1742 and reported, "The three little boys that were converted when I was last here came to me and wept and prayed with me before our Saviour. A minister tells me scarce one is fallen back that were awakened, both amongst old and young."

From 1874-1883 Children's prayer meetings sprang up following D. L. Moody's campaigns in Paisley, Greenock, and Mintlaw.

Charles Haddon Spurgeon endorsed the ministry of children. In April 1868, he advocated lively meetings for the young, with speakers, revival hymns, and 'The liberty of clapping hands and cheering every now and then.' He advocated prayer meetings for boys and girls and said, 'Never fear precocity, there is much more danger of indifference.' He believed children capable of doing their own outreach and of looking after each other pastorally. He concluded, 'We have never developed the capabilities of youth as we should have done.'

Wow! "We have never developed the capabilities of youth as we SHOULD have done". What a statement! As you can see in these journals from history, God has always had His hand on the children and wants so much more for them than coloring books and cookies during Sunday morning service! He obviously desires a relationship not only with us, but with every child on the face of the earth. He has plans for them, for their future, and for His Kingdom.

As we teach our children who they are, what they possess in Christ and how they can minister under His power and direction, we are going to see a sold-out army of kids leading the world to Jesus. Let us lead and encourage them so that they may impart wisdom, faith, and healing to thousands now and in years to come. Maybe in the future, someone will be reading accounts of YOUR child's experiences of revival and power.

KIDS CAN HEAR

Psalm 127:3 says, "Behold, children are a gift of the LORD, the fruit of the womb is a reward" (NASB). Unfortunately, many times adults think of them as too immature, too little, or not ready for the deeper things of God. A typical Sunday morning class might be teaching a Bible story, maybe doing a craft, singing a couple of songs, trying to memorize a Bible verse, and making sure they have their take home "hand out" as they run out the door. For a few kids, they will gain plenty of head knowledge, and might even be able to quote Scripture, but for the majority of the children, the material will be lost to them.

Why is this? Because they did not connect the "truth" they memorized with the person of Jesus. There was no encounter with Christ to further deepen and solidify their experience. In Jesus' parable of the sower and the seeds in Matthew 13:19, He says, "When anyone hears the word of the kingdom and does not understand it, the evil one comes and snatches away what has been sown in his heart."

There has to be a better way to bring children deeper into a relationship with God. How can we get kids to consistently and honestly seek after God and encounter Him? We want their lives to be changed, and for them to fully understand WHO God is, HOW He loves them, WHAT kind of power is available to them, WHEN they can access His presence, and WHY it's so much fun getting close to Jesus.

This can only be accomplished through relationship with the Father. It has to be more than just a corporate prayer at the beginning and end of class. Although grounding in the Word is vital for growth and necessary to nurture and maintain a healthy relationship with the Lord, it has to be more than head knowledge that they MIGHT or might not take away from the classes. Children need an intimate, close encounter with God that they just cannot get through lesson plans alone. They need to be taught how to sense His awesome presence, and be able to "tune in" to His voice.

We adults may be hearing God's voice for ourselves, but how did we learn to hear Him? When did we learn? More often than not, we had to discover His voice on our own, over many years, with little influence or direction from the outside. We may have read books, heard some great messages, maybe even tried having people pray for us, but most of us will probably admit that we had to stumble our way through to the Father's heart.

Children need to be taught how to go to Jesus on their own. They need to learn how to quiet themselves, come before God with praise and thanksgiving, ask Him to come be with them, and learn how to wait while listening and watching. They need to know what to expect in prayer, and what God's part is in that. Then, as they grow, it will become second nature to go to Jesus immediately when they have situations in life that they need help with.

But how can children hear the voice of God? Is it even possible? Don't they "wiggle" and "peek" too much? Are they not just too "antsy" to be able to sit and pray for more than 30 seconds? Certainly they must be more mature and "ready" to come into the very presence of the living God? I thought so myself for a very long time, until God literally knocked me off my feet by the prayers of children at a conference years ago. Then I began to understand His truth concerning these precious little warriors. Oh, how things have changed!

The first thing we need to realize is that these kids are no different in God's eyes than adults. In Acts 10:34, Peter is speaking to a group of believers and states: "Of a truth I perceive that God is no respecter of persons" (ASV). According to this statement, God does not show partiality, and He treats everyone on the same basis. God includes children in everything because they are to be in His presence, too.

In the Hebrew culture, the children were taught by participation and example how to listen for God, how to worship Him, and how to pray. We need to include our kids in our worship and prayer times, and teach them the ways of God, also. This is God's idea and command, not man's. Deuteronomy 6:7 says, "You shall teach them diligently to your children, and shall talk of them when you sit in your house, and when you walk by the way, and when you lie down, and when you rise" (NASB). God speaks through the prophet in Joel 2:16 about convening a solemn assembly – an important meeting for the people - and says, "Gather the people, sanctify the congregation, assemble the elders, gather the children and the nursing infants" (NASB). When the people gather, even for important meetings, the children are to be included. God does not "cull them out".

He goes on in Joel 2:28 to say, "It will come about after this that I will pour out My Spirit on all mankind; and your sons and daughters will prophesy, your old men will dream dreams and your young men will see visions" (NASB). When God says "all mankind", He MEANS "ALL mankind"! He's very direct and explicit that the young are to be involved.

God promises to pour out on our children as well as the adults, and that is exciting to me. We see His importance on kids reflected everywhere in Scripture just by His using the title for all those who believe in Him as His "children" and He as our "Father". Certainly God, in all His wisdom, could have called them something else!

Children are used throughout Scripture as examples. There is the story of Abraham and Issac, Elijah and the widow's son, David and Goliath, all the children healed by Jesus in the New Testament, and many more. Even the fact that Jesus was born and grew up as a child shows us God's importance on the issue of children. He didn't come as an adult, but as a child.

The emphasis God places on children is obvious and unmistakable. Jesus Himself made this point when the disciples were attempting to move the children out of His way in Mark 10: 13-16

"And they were bringing children to him that he might touch them, and the disciples rebuked them. But when Jesus saw it, he was INDIGNANT and said to them, "Let the children come to me; do not hinder them, for to such belongs the kingdom of God. Truly, I say to you, whoever does not receive the kingdom of God like a child shall not enter it." And he took them in his arms and blessed them, laying his hands on them" (ESV).

Indignant? That's not a word I would readily associate with Jesus! Webster's dictionary defines indignant as "feeling or showing anger because of something unjust or unworthy". In other words, Jesus was really upset with the disciples about their attitude. His point was that these children have a purpose – read into this, Disciples! There is an importance here that cannot be hidden away under a coloring book.

Notice what Mark goes on to say in verse 16: "He took them in His arms and blessed them, laying His hands on them." What a picture of the Father heart of God! One thing I believe He was trying to show the disciples was a huge principle of the importance of children and their place in the Kingdom. Nowhere else in Scripture do we see Jesus actually laying His hands on anyone and blessing them.

There had to be something special about being a child that Jesus Himself would place such emphasis on it. Why did they have to become "like a child" to enter into the kingdom of God? What lesson was Jesus teaching them that He would use a child as an example? Could it be their purity and innocence, their trusting heart, their complete faith in their father? I believe it is for these reasons and so much more that Jesus finds children to be a great example for us today. Children DO have something to give to the kingdom – they DO have a part.

The story of one of the little girls in our kid's ministry is a good example of how children can learn to trust in God. Samantha's family was "babysitting" a pet iguana for some friends while they were away. They would feed it, play with it, and care for it everyday. I'm not a lizard fan, but am quite sure the kids loved having it around! One day, when Samantha went in to feed the iguana, she found it lifeless and cold, it's head in it's water bowl. Of course, it scared her, but her poor little heart just ached for this pet. Her mother came in and tried to console her, but Samantha just wouldn't accept that it was gone.

This was a time in our ministry we had been teaching the kids about trusting in God, especially in prayer. We had told them that whatever you asked God for, trusting in Him and believing, He would do for you, regardless what it was (Matt 21:21-22) – just believe. There had been many opportunities during our Children's Church to "practice the Presence" and believe. Samantha took this to heart and began praying life into that lizard. She cried and asked God to bring the creature back to life because the family would miss their pet and it shouldn't have died. What happened next took them both by surprise.

The iguana took a breath. Now, Samantha's mom wasn't sure if that was just the "finale" of his life, or if something was happening, so she watched more intently. He took another breath, and Samantha, not noticing this, kept on praying and interceding compassionately for its life. Then they both saw his tail move, and then a leg, and finally, he opened his eyes and started moving around. Samantha was overjoyed, and when her mom was able to breathe, checked out the creature from stem to stern, finding everything in good working order.

Samantha completely trusted in God to do what she asked, because she knew from experience and practice that God loved her and would hear her prayer. To this day I still find it incredible that in that moment of despair and pain, she cried out to God for help rather than give in to what seemed like the inevitable. Oh, that we would learn from her example!

Ok, so God sets the same importance on kids as He does adults. Great. I still didn't quite get that until I heard David and Kathie Walters, authors, speakers, and children's equippers, minister at a children's conference years ago. They made a statement that rocked my world. "When children come to Jesus, they don't receive a junior Holy Spirit. They get the whole thing." Wow! They don't get a tiny little Holy Spirit at conversion. They get the whole package because God is not a respecter of persons. God wants children to have the same intimate, loving relationship of guidance, filling, indwelling and power that we enjoy. What a concept!

This revelation became increasingly clearer as I studied, prayed, and interacted with the kids in my own ministry. God CAN speak to children, and they CAN hear. Take, for example, the story of Samuel. As a child, he slept in the Temple at night. Part of his job was tending the oil lamps and candles, making sure they never went out. Being in the very presence of God in the Temple on a continual basis produced this effect on Samuel: I Sam 2:26 says, "Now the boy Samuel was growing in stature and in favor both with the LORD and with men" (NASB).

As the story goes on in I Samuel 3:1-19, Samuel heard God's voice three times, but needed Eli to explain to him what he was hearing. We, also, need to instruct and direct children to be able to hear His voice. Samuel then was privy to a huge adult-sized download from God. Would God have entrusted Israel's future to a little boy? Yes, but only to a child who was spending time in His presence and was listening and obeying. Since God is the same yesterday, today and forever, can He not do that today with OUR children? 1 Sam 3:19, "Thus Samuel grew and the LORD was with him and let none of his words fail" (NASB). I want to help raise a whole army of Samuels by connecting them with the Father and then watch them make history.

So how is this actually done? How do you bring a child into the very presence of God? Is there a switch you can flip on and off as they walk into your room at church? No, but you can understand and prepare them for their encounter with Jesus. Over the years of trial and error, praying and studying, watching and (dare I say it) "experimenting" with this concept, God has shown how He loves to reach His little ones and how they do, indeed, experience God, feel His touch, and hear His loving voice. The scores of reports today of children hearing and seeing Jesus during medical crisis, in dreams, and in countless other situations are overwhelming in their implications.

Pastor Todd Burpo recounts his son Colton's experiences of going to Heaven during emergency surgery in the book, "Heaven Is For Real". As a four year old, Colton had never seen or known his great grandfather, but was able to pick him out of a picture after this experience, telling his parents he spoke with him in Heaven. Colton also was able to tell them about his sister who was miscarried before he was born, although his parents had never spoken about her. He talks about seeing Jesus and John the Baptist. How can we explain this without acknowledging that God speaks to and uses children?

How can we rationalize a 6 year old girl praying over a man she's never met and telling him God wants him to take the job he's been praying about? In this instance, during a mission trip to a neighboring state, the man in question thought it was "cute" that little kids would pray for him. He was in total amazement as he told us afterwards with tears in his eyes, "I didn't even tell my wife I was considering this job. How did she know that?" When he asked the little intercessor, she just looked at him plain as day and sweetly said, "Cause Jesus told me". Kids have their part in God's plan for us – not only in ministry, but to teach us as well!

Bringing children into the presence of God is such an awesome, and actually, pretty easy process to be a part of. Of course, OUR hearts need to be right with Him before we can take our kids down that path. How can we take them somewhere we have never been ourselves? This is a great time to work together with the children we're training, learning ourselves as we grow. As we go deeper with Jesus, spending time in His presence, gleaning from His glory, it makes it easier to sense the flow of God and how to introduce that to the children. Developing our own quiet times with the Lord, time in both the Word and His presence, are vital to the success of bringing your children before the Creator.

When you spend time with God, in prayer and waiting on Him, you pick up the very essence of Jesus, who and what He is. Kids are drawn to that. Did you ever wonder why the children wanted to be around Jesus? Children don't want to hang out with boring or bland people. That very reason is why I think our Lord had a great personality and laughed – a lot! We are brought up to think of Jesus as quiet, forlorn, no smile, serious all the time. When I think about Him with children, I can picture a man happy with the kids, joking with them, loving on them, looking them in the eye, and KNOWING them. I believe the essence of Jesus drew them to Himself.

God wants to form relationships with ALL His "kids"! If He gives us, young and old, the Holy Spirit to flow through our lives and help us grow in Him, should we not allow the children to learn and grown right along beside us? It is our responsibility to take them along with us on this journey and "train them up in the way they should go" Proverbs 22:6 (NASB).

First we need to prepare their hearts. Teaching them on their level about the ways to connect, talk with and hear from God is essential. Don't dumb it down, but keep it at their level. Kids are pretty smart, especially when it comes to things of the Spirit. We are a spirit inside of a body (I Thess 5:23), and I like to believe that their little spirits communed with God before they were even born There was relationship there for Jeremiah 1:5 says, "Before I formed you in the womb, I knew you. Before you were born, I consecrated you!"

From my experience, children actually have an easier time coming to Jesus than adults. These kids, being young, have not had the garbage of the world's cares and responsibilities laid on them yet. They are practically a blank slate. Their innate innocence and purity opens them up quite easily to God. Jesus is drawn to innocence and purity (Matt 5:8) – He LOVES it! So it makes even more sense that He would respond to these little ones. They don't have the walls that many of us, as adults, have built up over time.

Teaching about prayer is always a first for groups of little ones who've had little introduction into that. What it is, why we do it, how Jesus will respond, and the words we might use. Kids are constantly watching us as we worship and pray, whether we know it or not! They pick up on WHAT we're doing and saying, but don't always know WHY we do or say it. We need to explain to our precious young ones how important communication with God really is, and how much fun it can become. They need to know about Jesus' prayer life and the things He talked to His father about. It's a model they can understand.

We need to teach children about the different postures in prayer – kneeling, standing, sitting, lying on the floor. Use Scripture to give examples and back up the importance of each and when they might be used. Encourage them that there is no right or wrong way to get "situated" before God, just be comfortable. I tell them that their posture may change as they spend more time with Jesus. I also speak to them about things such as the lifting of hands, and what that means. We take time to try each posture, sometimes in a "game mode", so they become comfortable with changing positions and understanding why these are important.

Sometimes God will move on them in different ways, so children also need to be taught about the various things they may "feel or sense" during these times of prayer. To head off fear or uncertainty, it's important to explain what they might experience in His presence. Do we risk having them "make up" these feelings? Yes, but understand that as these children begin to develop their "prayer muscles", they want to feel a part of the group, and they may say or do things at first that help them be included. It will pass. We never discount a child's experience. That could "dam up" the child's attempts and create doubt. We guide, encourage growth, and just don't give a lot of attention to those things that are obviously not of God. Once they "get in the zone", everything else falls away when the reality of Jesus' presence sets in!

We could speak to them about getting a "funny feeling in your stomach". Your spirit originates in that area, and if God wants to "love on you", He might start there. I will explain to them that Jesus has more love to put into us than sometimes what our human bodies can take, so we might shake a little with all that power inside us! I keep it light, sometimes with a little humor added, to help them feel comfortable and relaxed. Jesus is gentle and loves His little ones, and creating a frightening picture will not be conducive to the prayer/worship time.

We also talk about how they might feel like crying or laughing, and that these are ways our bodies react to being touched by Jesus and His love. I constantly reassure them with a smile that all these things are normal and ok, and that God will never scare or hurt us. It is just a different way of being "loved on" than our moms and dads do.

There needs to be discussion on how some people might smell things, feel a touch, or experience tingling in their hands or arms. Of course, we also spend time on things that God might SHOW them, like pictures, "little movies", words, numbers, etc. All this creates expectation in their spirits, quells any fear, and really explains to them what happens so they're prepared and not surprised. It is necessary to continually remind them that they could experience any of these things, or none of these things. I tell them that God does what HE wants, and touches us all in different ways, so it is not really as important "what you get" as "WHO you get"!

We have had children, for instance, who, during prayer, have seen Jesus and them swinging on a swing, playing in a field, or just sitting on the sofa and being held. Kids get excited when they share with you about Jesus patting their head or holding their hand during prayer times. I've had children smell apples, roses, and bread. I've seen children from troubled homes with tears running down their faces during prayer, then have them tell me later that Jesus kept saying that He loves them. Many children will hear Jesus call their name, or speak to them about their behavior. He WANTS to talk to His children – and when they listen expectantly, they hear.

God gave me a great tidbit that is always shared with any group of "newbies". I tell them that there are eyes and ears on their heart (Eph 1:18) – that those eyes or ears were made to see or hear only Jesus. While they are learning to pray and listen for Him to speak, it might take time to be trained to identify His voice, but it will happen! If you present this right, those children will be already "tuning in" to see if they hear anything before you even start praying.

We will share with them that God will never scare you when He talks with you, or say anything Jesus wouldn't say. If they hear something that they think is wrong, mean, scary, or isn't what they think they'd find in the Bible, it's probably just the devil trying to trick them. If that happens, they just tell him to go away and according to the Bible, he has to. James 4:7 "Be subject therefore unto God; but resist the devil, and he will flee from you" (ASV). I very rarely have had any problems in that area.

Creating expectation in these precious spirits is important. They need to understand that they are about to hear from the Creator of the universe, and that He has something very special to speak to them about that no one else will hear! You might want to ask them, "Who wants to visit with Jesus today?" You might be surprised at the number of children who respond.

I will also remind the kids that for God to honor us coming to Him, we need to remember that He loves obedience. We need to be obedient to those people in authority (that would be you). He will honor the fact that you are obeying, and then come a little closer. Therefore, you might say, if your leaders tell you to keep your eyes closed, you need to be obedient in that, no matter what is going on around you. God will make sure you get your reward for being obedient (Heb 11:6).

I encourage them to keep their eyes shut so they won't become "distracted". Being distracted, like looking to see what everyone else is doing, or wiggling around a lot, keeps us from seeing Jesus and hearing His voice. So if they really, really want to hear Him, they need to be very still with their eyes shut just focusing on and thinking about Him. I keep my eyes open during these prayer times, at least at the start, and watch the children while they're getting "settled". If they open their eyes, I will point to my own eyes and then to them, motioning for them to close their eyes. There will be a few that need the extra reminders, but eventually, their eyes will remain closed. Most children will be able to do this for a short time to start with, and some will need several sessions, but I have experienced children eventually being able to quiet themselves.

It is important to note here that the focus be on Jesus. Focusing on anything else draws attention away from the Lord and may even lead to distorted experiences, opening doors that are better left shut. This is something that you do not need to be afraid of, but watching and praying. You can hear His voice – trust the children to be able to, also, with a few reminders.

There may be one or two that might not seem to "get it", but don't worry about them – Jesus has them in His sights! It's a timing and maturing thing that will eventually work out. Try to keep those children quiet and in position throughout your session, and eventually they'll pick it up by just being in His presence as He shows up.

Some of you are thinking, "Ah, this is all well and good, but how do you get them to sit still?" Here are some tips I've learned on that subject. Chairs are notorious for causing distractions, and are not completely necessary for kids at this stage. I pull out all my chairs and have them sit on the floor. Kids are more comfortable there anyway, especially if you sit with them. Of course, a rug or carpet is nice, but sitting on the floor is so much more their "turf". Have them find a spot where they won't be touching anyone else. I might even move several of them if I see they will become distracted by friends who are nearby. After they master this stage, and you begin to see progress, eventually they will enter in and hear His voice anywhere – on a chair, in a car, in the backyard, etc.

Music is a huge part of this learning process for kids. The right music has the anointing to calm, help focus, and deepen their growing experience with Jesus. God created music as a way for us to come into His presence and worship Him. The enemy has turned it around, distorted it, and tried to give it back to us. We need to be especially careful of what we are presenting in the form of music to our children. They are sensitive little creatures, and pick up on stuff pretty quickly.

I would choose Christian music that is proven in your own quiet times with the Lord, and from good, solid sources. There are many CD's out there today that are not the best choices for their quiet times. Check their publishers, read the backs of cases, listen and listen again, ask God to give you wisdom, all proven to help decipher what is food for our little warriors and what is "confusion". I have included a page of "resources" at the end of this book as a suggested list of music to start with.

I almost always use music in the early stages of bringing kids into His presence. It creates an atmosphere, along with the teaching, to help children sense God's presence. It's not an absolute necessity, but I have found it's an awesome tool. We use totally instrumental music in the beginning, because in helping children focus, the words can just get in the way. Eventually, you may be able to use songs with lyrics.

When it finally comes time to "practice the presence of God" (because we get better and better at it as we practice, of course!), we need to start with everyone in their position on the floor. We will explain how we are going to talk to and see Jesus, then be able to just "soak" in His presence and let Him love on them!

We explain that soaking is just like a sponge. When we pour water on a sponge, it soaks up the water and holds it for a long time. As we "soak" in Jesus, we get more and more of Him inside us, then we just sit and hold it for a long time. I will tell them it is kind of like taking a bath. When you sit in the tub and the water is warm, you can relax and it feels really good. I compare that with soaking in Jesus – it is a time when you can relax and be with Jesus. He will make you warm (feel good) all over and you will be cleaner when you get out!

Make sure they're in a comfortable, safe area on the floor, then they may be encouraged to take a deep breath and let it out slowly, perhaps a couple of times. Again they're reminded to keep their eyes closed, and if I see one "peeking", I will point to my eyes and to them. I may need to do this for several sessions as they're learning what's expected of them, but eventually, they will comply.

We may start the music low, and I will keep my voice low, too, to encourage focus. The Word says to enter His gates with thanksgiving and His courts with praise, so I may tell them we will take a few moments to thank Him for things. They are led in a few ideas to get the ball rolling, and then told to thank God for those things in their mind. I tell them to see the things, like mom and dad, nice room, clothes, etc, and then thank God for those things.

After a few minutes, I tell them we will take some time to praise Him. We verbally list a few things, such as praising Him for being so kind and compassionate, for being the great Creator, or for being such a merciful God. Then, again, they must think of things on their own and praise Him for that in their minds. Again, we encourage them to see those things, and then praise Him for them in their minds. The children need to learn to do this on their own, and they can! Believe that God will move on them, and He will!

After a few more moments, still telling them quietly to keep their eyes closed and try to be still, it's time to hear from Jesus. We will invite them to listen with the "ears on their heart", and to listen for a voice that will be inside them rather than with the ears on their head! These thoughts might sound like an idea or words that come to their mind. Remember, we have set the stage, provided the time for them to meet with Jesus, and trust He will do what He says He will do - James 4:8 "Draw near to God and He will draw near to You" (ESV). We have to have faith now that Jesus will do His part. He's always shown up in our meetings, and the children love that.

I may start this "quiet time" with a prayer and invite the Lord to move on His kids. There's not a lot of other verbal speaking during this time, unless it's necessary to quietly remind them to stop wiggling more and keep their eyes shut. I try not to say anything too much during this time, but might walk around and touch a child, rearranging him if necessary, to accommodate the "atmosphere".

The first and second time I do this with a new group, I will keep the soaking time down to about 6 -7 minutes, adjusting time slightly for either a receptive or a hesitant response. Every group is different, and what works for one may not work for another. Make sure you do allow plenty of time, however, as we're giving JESUS time to touch the children and wait appropriately for their response! Jesus loves having His children (of ALL ages) in this position, coming to Him, so He will show up.

The key here is to be tuned in and sensitive to what God is doing with your children. You may have one or two that will have a difficult time, and you may have one or two that fall right into Jesus' arms! I don't interrupt a child unless I see they are having a hard time or might be afraid. Then I would quietly go and talk with them, again, staying tuned in and receptive to what is needed at the time. Many times I will sit and pray silently over the children, always staying focused on Jesus and asking Him what He wants to do next. I pray for the children, asking God to reveal Himself to them in a tangible way, on their level.

After the first introductory sessions, we will increase the amount of time they spend in prayer by maybe 5-10 minutes each session, according to how they respond. Once the children have the "hang of it", it's going to be second nature for them to go to their spot and ready themselves for their time with the Lord. What an awesome, beautiful thing it is to see kids go expectantly before the Father. I love watching children hear from Jesus and see their reactions – they're never the same again. In our ministry, we sometimes have had soaking sessions of up to three hours at a stretch, with the kids always asking for more. God moves powerfully during these times, and sometimes we can see His hand on the kids as they wait on Him.

At the end of each session, we will turn the music down but not off. It keeps the atmosphere softened and nice for the kids to come out of their prayer time. We will gather them quietly together on the carpet, and sit with them to have our "processing" time. This is vital to gauge what is happening with your children and get feedback.

It will be a time of teaching, encouraging, and clearing up things that were heard, seen, or felt. It also gives the children who did not receive anything a chance to see that Jesus DOES show up, and to reassure them that they, too, will experience Jesus soon! Kids need this sounding board time, and to do this with them in a group is very encouraging, as one child usually reinforces what another experienced.

I ask the children first off to raise their hands if anyone felt they "met with Jesus" during their prayer time. There are always hands up. I also ask, in succession, who felt something, heard something, smelled something, saw anything, etc. They are told that they need to be honest about raising their hands - you might not have received anything this time, but you probably will next time.

We explain that hearing from Jesus and being touched by Him is like walking for the first time when you are a baby. You did not just get up and walk – you had to practice, because it was something new, like riding a bike. It is the same way with hearing from Jesus – you keep "practicing the presence of Jesus" until you finally get there! He's always with us and around us, but we need to get those ears on our heart tuned to hear him, and sometimes that takes a little bit of time. Reassurance at this point is crucial, as some children just learning this could become discouraged that they didn't experience anything the first time.

Once we have raised the hands (and you might be surprised, again), then we go through each sense and talk more about it. Who "felt" something? What did you feel? Was it scary or was it ok? If scary, we discuss it and try to determine what was happening. Most kids have a great experience.

Sometimes, due to home situations, misinformation, or just plain enemy interference, there might be some fear. Reassurance, a hug, and a smile go very far.

We will discuss each sensory experience with almost the same questions and ask them to talk about it with the group. This will help to alleviate most fears and curiosities. We allow others to ask questions or comment within reason. Sometimes we laugh a little (eases tensions and relaxes them), and if necessary, we take a moment to re-teach something that was not clear.

I try to keep this time, dependant on group number, down to about 5 minutes. I always ask the kids at the end, "Would you like to do this again sometime"? Most children will raise their hands, and even verbalize their "hunger". I have observed with kids that once they make that experiential connection, they are "hooked" and will love to come back again into the presence of Jesus.

There is always time to explain to the children that this awesome feeling of being with and listening to Jesus can be done at any time. We tell them that you can talk to Him when you are in corporate worship at church, riding in your car, sitting under a tree, before going to bed at night, and even taking a bath! We encourage the kids to try to talk to Jesus again in the next day or two on their own, quieting themselves, thanking and praising Him, then asking Him to come talk to them and waiting, listening and watching. It's great when they come back with reports of where they were and what was said as they venture out on their own.

After 3-4 times in these "soaking sessions", your children will automatically know what to do and how to prepare themselves for their prayer time. It will become second nature to find their spot, prepare their hearts, thank and praise Him, then listen with the ears of their heart for His familiar voice. As time goes on, you will see where you will need to fine tune your particular group. You may need to go over some of the material again as a follow up, or just have a question and answer time with your kids if there is an exceeding amount of questions. There may be one or two of your children who are having a hard time with the process and need some one on one time during your sessions. Most children, however, can tune in very well after several sessions and can really begin to respond.

What do you do with the things they are getting? I encourage all my kids to keep a notebook, a journal, of what God is telling them. We will take time during class to write out things or draw pictures, and try to include the date, day and time they received them. It's a great tool for them to be able to go back and verify things they felt God say or do. Sometimes we let them pray specifically for an event, person or group, or situation that needs attention.

These kids hear the most amazing things, and writing it down solidifies that experience for them.

Parents especially love this journaling, as they can watch their child's progress and interact with them at home. We encourage children to share what they have received from the Lord with their parents. It's an opportunity to bring the family in on their encounters, to encourage, verify or help gently correct things, and make a real impact on the family. I've actually had parents tell me THEIR walk with God had grown due to their children's experiences.

We take children (6-12 year olds) on mission trips across the country each year. During this time, one of our requirements is spending time with Jesus each night before we go to sleep. This quiets their hearts and minds down and allows them time to hear His words for them which continue after they fall asleep. They are required to write these thoughts down in their trip journal, along with thoughts during the day that might arise, and afterwards they have a nice file of information about how God moved on them during their trip.

One of the things I love about what kids get is the insight it gives me into their little lives. It's awesome to watch God change a life week by week, month by month, year by year, and then look back at where they started from. You can see how God is working in their lives, and what their spiritual giftings might be. When there are issues in their lives they need to deal with, you are able to communicate with them better and help them "go to Jesus" for the answers.

Leading children into a deep relationship with Jesus is so rewarding and fun. They grow, become stronger, and go on to make godly choices for their lives because Jesus has become their Friend, Guide and Counselor. Once these children are in His presence, equipped, ready and soaking up the "more" of Jesus, I get to just sit back, watch and marvel at how much our God loves His kids and counts them as equals in His Kingdom.

KIDS
CAN DO!

As my two daughters were growing up, there were many times I was nervous about things they were doing, and rightly so. I remember being very watchful as they crossed the street, walked down the sidewalk, drove a car for the first time, and went on trips by themselves, etc. Those were days when their safety was the main issue.

In other activities, with careful monitoring and some teaching involved, my young girls were able to accomplish several things by themselves which gave them confidence and boosted their self-esteem. Even though it may have been deemed more difficult for a child, they baked treats to sell at our yard sales, organized and held "craft classes" in our home for neighborhood kids, made three course dinners for Daddy, planted and grew tomatoes for themselves (Allen and I hated tomatoes!), and much more. We all help our children to do things that are important, such as cleaning their rooms and doing chores, but we need to allow and encourage them to go further!

The Word says that we are to "train them up in the way they should go" (Prov. 22:6). That doesn't just mean raise them in the fear and admonition of the Lord. It also means asking, "What direction are you sending them in, Lord? What do You want to do with their life? What will they become, and how can I begin to pour into them now? How can we be preparing them for the personal assignments You have for them both now and in the future? It's our responsibility, as parents and as children's leaders, to pray and ask God for vision to see what their little spirits need to equip them for what's coming in their lives.

We don't usually get the whole picture, because it's not necessary that we know every detail. It would be great if God told us, "Tommy will be a doctor and live in California and find the cure for cancer". We're usually just given something like, "Tommy has a healing anointing on his life". The details come, little by little with each passing year, as their specific assignments from God begin to take shape. God will, however, give us a "sneak peek" of what's coming up in their lives…if we ask Him.

We all watch as our children grow, attend school, maybe go off to college and become adults, but do we have to wait until they are grown to discover the general plan God has for them? Does God wait until they are adults to formulate their assignments? I think not. Psalm 139:16 says, "Your eyes saw my unformed substance; in your book were written, every one of them, the days that were formed for me, when as yet there was none of them". Before our children were born, God knew them and had a plan for them. If He entrusted them to us, as their parents and leaders, why would He not want us to "feed them" and prepare them for their coming work? Isn't that what God calls us to do? We need to ask the Lord to show us generally where our children are headed, and then begin to take them down that road. There is not a "too early" stage for this.

I really like Psalm 127:4 which states, "Like arrows in the hand of a warrior are the children of one's youth". Which directions will that arrow go when released? Will it hit the mark or fall short? Archery had to be very precise because, when in battle the warriors' lives and the lives of others depended upon it. If they did not aim correctly, or they were careless, the arrow would not complete the job it was created for. Like an arrow, children need guidance and direction to become effective instruments in God's hands, and to complete His will in many different situations. Childhood is the time to begin training children to be what God has called them to be! What "arrows" do you have in your ministry or family, and how are they being developed today?

Listen to Isaiah 49:2: "He hath made me a polished shaft (or arrow); in His quiver hath He kept me close" (ASV). The archer takes time to precisely fashion the arrow, finely grinding and polishing the head until it is shaped exactly the way it needs to be. He works the shaft of the arrow until it is perfectly straight. He also takes the time to wind the thread around the feathers. They will help guide the arrow in the correct direction. Great care is taken in making these weapons of warfare. Isaiah also says, "in His quiver hath He kept me close". There is a protecting, a "hiding away" in Him until the time comes to be sent out.

Children are those arrows. With Jesus' leading, we work with them to shape and define who they are called to be. We sharpen them by taking them with us into the presence of God, feeding them the things they need to grow spiritually, and encouraging them along the way. Finally, the moment comes when God says, "Ok, now it's YOUR turn to fly". That child is pulled from the quiver, aimed and released. Hopefully, fully equipped and ready to complete the mission the Father selected for them.

In Psalm 144:12, David praises God for the things He does for His children. He invokes prayers of blessings by saying, "May our sons in their youth be like plants full grown, our daughters like corner pillars cut for the structure of a palace". His praise concludes with, "Blessed are the people to whom such blessings fall! Blessed are the people whose God is the LORD!" It's a blessing to have sons who are like plants full grown while still in their youth. It's a blessing to have daughters who, while still young, are strong in spirit and accomplish things usually meant for the "more mature". Let's believe God that He will "do far more abundantly above all that we ask or think, according to the power at work within" our children!

Once we have a picture of what direction God is taking our kids, it's easy to train and prepare them! I was ministering with Sarah Turner as an assistant children's leader in a church some time ago, when three boys came to us separately, each with a question. The first young man, about 10 or 11 years old, came to us and said, "I really want to play the drums." A musician myself, I was excited, but I didn't know anything about teaching him to play drums. We told him to pray for God to lead him, talk with his parents, get a pair of drumsticks and just start tapping out rhythms wherever he could. I was praying his parents could provide him some drum lessons.

The next young man, about the same age, came to us several weeks later. I had forgotten all about the first one, until he asked the same question, except he wanted to play the bass. Again, we told him to pray for direction, talk with his parents, and see what God would do. The third boy came to us shortly thereafter, asking about playing electric guitar. We told him the same thing. Each of these kids was very adamant about playing these instruments and, interestingly enough, they had not been speaking to each other about doing this.

Within about a month, the bass player had been given a bass and shown a few notes. The drummer and the guitar players had also been given instruments, all from different sources and at different times. They were all very excited and began practicing individually on the few notes and chords that they learned. They picked up a few pointers from our worship band guys, but no formal lessons were being given at that time.

Within another couple of months, they all came to us again asking if they could start a worship band, and would we help them? Sarah and I were perplexed – we had never heard of children this young doing anything like this – we did not know of any manuals, or books that we could read on how to do this. So, we prayed and asked for guidance and felt God's leading to work with them and that God would bless it and show us what to do. My husband, Allen, and I, both being musicians, began regular rehearsal times. We gave them songs that had the chords and notes they already knew. Within several weeks, we had at least six or seven other children asking to do various things with our "band". We had a flute player, keyboardist, singers, and even our own sound man, who was only age 13 or 14 at the time.

Four to five months later, our "kids worship band" was leading children's church worship on Sunday mornings, and they were great! They had their own repertoire of eight or more songs, and, as time went on, they were always learning more. We continued to rehearse with them weekly, amazed at how quickly they learned and by the skill they had at such a young age! After a couple of hours of training with our sound technician, they could also set up and tear down their own audio system and do a sound check before service all by themselves.

Eventually, these kids would go with us on their first children's mission trip. They ministered together as a team, leading heart felt worship with excellence, and bringing the presence of God into every room we ministered in. There was such an anointing on these little worshipers! Through our rehearsals, our times together in prayer and our teaching about worship, these kids knew what they were bringing to the table in any service they were in. Sarah and I would just sit back, awed at what God had done in such a short time. To me, it was as if God was saying, "Don't ever underestimate what I can do with My children." This was totally God working, not us; so we cannot take any credit for something so incredibly Him, but we learned so much!

It is important to note that we did not reject their beginning desires as an impossibility or tell them they could not do that because of their youth. We were always openly looking for what God's direction was, praying and watching, then moving forward a little at a time. God did all the rest. When we thought we had gone as far as we could with them, God showed us more and gave us the resources to complete His plan. Today those original boys are all majorly gifted musicians, with hearts turned toward God in all they do. We gave them a platform to walk out what God was calling them to, and we believed in them. We helped those arrows to be prepared for God's use.

God moved in the same way with other areas of ministry. There were children who were interested in dance; so we brought in a teacher who had Jesus' heart, both for kids, and for anointed, God-focused dance. We saw amazing things happen. The dance troupe grow to almost 20 children (including both boys and girls). They were taught WHY we dance, with Scriptural references, Biblical examples and more. We saw them transform into true worshippers at a very young age. They understood what they were doing. It wasn't just because it was fun. There was meaning and depth to it, and they LOVED that!

These children also went on kids' mission trips. They danced in parks, on the street, in malls, halfway houses, and more. Everywhere they went, they carried the heart and message of Jesus, and people wept and were touched by God. Not only were these young worshippers displaying His glory and proclaiming His name, but they were ministering healing and seeds of salvation to everyone who watched.

Eventually, the dance group also began ministering with flags of all sizes. They were trained on what the different colors represented and Scriptural basis for using flags. They knew what they were saying to people, and they prayed over every flag, music selection, and opportunity God gave them. It was an amazing thing to be in their presence when they moved under the anointing of the Holy Spirit!

In another church, our children's ministry was also full of promising young lives. I can remember during my personal prayer times praying over each boy and girl, asking God to reveal His plans for that particular child. I would ask Him what He wanted me to pour into them corporately and individually. Then I listened for His direction and watched the children for confirming signs of what I felt I had been told.

Over a period of a year, God tuned me in to His plans for many of these children. Some were pretty obvious, and others took a little time, but I was able to see them as Jesus saw them. In a few cases, I was shown issues that needed to be prayerfully and carefully worked on. During other times, I just wept with joy as He showed me the purity of a future leader and His joy over them. I had never experienced that level of insight into children, and I was blown away by God's answer to my prayers for these, His little ones.

At one point, God told me to take each child out to a meal and spend several hours with them at least once a year. This individual attention not only made them feel very special and created a great amount of trust between us, but it also gave me the time to really get to know them – their interests, questions, fears and where they were in their walk with Jesus. I also began to see more of their path in life – the things their hearts longed for in a good way. I saw strengths and weaknesses, and I was given plans of how to encourage, feed, and build up their lives for the future works their Father was calling them to. It was an amazing time of revelation. Now I spend the time, to stay tuned in to what God is doing in their lives by taking "my kids" out at least once a year.

As I began to see what their abilities were and what God was calling each of them into, it was then easier to form a plan of action to resource what He was doing with them. There were no books or manuals on how to do this at that time. However, as I rested in Jesus and asked Him for direction, He never failed us! Our children's ministry took on a different look, as we began turning over more responsibilities to them.

We created "departments" such as audio/visual, where children were responsible for running the music, and operating a camcorder for video and pictures. We had an Intercessors' group with kids praying for the children's church service each week ahead of time, and listening for God's leading about things in our ministry. There was an ushers department, which was responsible for collecting and praying over our offering each week, helping visitors fill out cards and being their "buddy" for that day. We also had someone who became our "editor" for a quarterly newsletter. She was taught how to use the computer, gather information, and operate a program to build and publish the newsletter.

Each department had a department "head" who would be permanent, but would choose different ones each week to help, thus "mentoring" the children under them. When the department heads were getting to an age where they would be moving up to Jr. High ministry, they had to pray for, select, mentor, and finally, appoint a successor (with our oversight) before they could move on. It was self-propagating.

We had department meetings once a month, and usually the children chosen were seen as future leaders with an interest and/or skill in the area they worked in. This gave us, as adult leaders, the opportunity to closely monitor, pour into and gently lead these children into being the leaders they were called to be. One of the best parts of this whole process was that once they moved up into the Jr. High or High School youth groups, they already had skills and training to be a leader and could contribute on a much deeper and higher level. The leaders that received these kids recognized their growth and maturity and were excited to be able to "plug them in" quickly.

We would utilize as many resources as we could in their training. The audio/visual head, for example, would work with the adult sound department, being mentored by leaders with experience and a healthy walk with the Lord. These adults would become friends with our "future leader", and would walk them through the ins and outs of their department. Occasionally, this child would be asked to take pictures or video during an adult service. Afterwards, they would review them together. The adult would look for good points to praise and make corrections as necessary. If the mentor spent enough time training, eventually, the child would be ready to step into place in any adult service and do that job with excellence.

If children are given responsibilities, given encouragement - a "building up", and made to feel like they are worthy of that responsibility, you will see things that you have never thought possible. Through consistent pats on the back along with gentle correction and explanations - God will work through that child and amazing results will happen! If he/she is told, "Yes, you CAN do that", it WILL happen! Isn't that how our loving Father trains and encourages us? We need to pass that example on down to our children.

Of course, all this process must be bathed in prayer and the leader must listen closely for God's leading, being open to all possibilities and not putting God, or the kids, in a box. God is unique. He sometimes stretches us with some of the things He asks us to do. Are we flexible enough and obedient enough to move with His will instead of saying, "Oh, we've never done it that way before"? Do we trust God enough to be able to say, "Well, I've never seen anything like this, but I could try it and see what happens"? Do we believe that God can move on children? Is it possible that, if we just relax and, in faith, open up our minds, that God will move in such a way on our kids that WE can learn from THEM?

Look at the life of David. He was a young child, working in his father's fields tending sheep. Already, his father must have thought much of this young lad. He trusted him to take the sheep out, sometimes miles from home, all alone, and BELIEVED IN HIM to care for part of the family income.

While David tended sheep, part of his job was to protect them from predators so that the sheep would remain safe. The Bible tells us about a time when young David encountered a bear and later, a lion attacking the sheep. I

Samuel explains how he was able to save his flocks by killing the bear and the lion. We know that David grew up to be "a man after God's own heart" – searching for God, worshipping Him continually and communing with Him; so, of course, God gave David strength and courage thereby causing him to win his battles. God was with David from his youth.

This experience in David's youth later gave him the basis for his extreme courage, boldness, and bravery in fighting Goliath.

1Samuel 17:45-47 : Then David said to the Philistine, "You come to me with a sword and with a spear and with a javelin, but I come to you in the name of the LORD of hosts, the God of the armies of Israel, whom you have defied. This day the LORD will deliver you into my hand, and I will strike you down and cut off your head. And I will give the dead bodies of the host of the Philistines this day to the birds of the air and to the wild beasts of the earth, that all the earth may know that there is a God in Israel, and that all this assembly may know that the LORD saves not with sword and spear. For the battle is the LORD's, and he will give you into our hand."

The same principles apply today to our own children. If they are taught to worship, spend time communing with God, are given encouragement, trust, and responsibility, and if they believe that "I can do this", they, too, will be equipped with what they need when they need it. They can "do the stuff" with authority, boldness, and a solid trust in God.

We have to stop thinking of children as totally weak and helpless. God sees these "young warriors" in a completely different way than we do. When Samuel was looking for the next king among Jesse's sons, he was looking at the wrong thing. God corrected not only Samuel, but us as well!

1Samuel 16:7 "But the LORD said to Samuel, 'Do not look on his appearance or on the height of his stature, because I have rejected him. For the LORD sees not as man sees: man looks on the outward appearance, but the LORD looks on the heart.' "

The Lord is always looking for those who will complete His plans and serve Him. He's not necessarily looking for the strong in physical power, but for those whose eyes are fixed on Him and are willing to step out in obedience. David trusted God with his whole heart, and God loved that! Even though he was young, his heart was abandoned to God; so, God gave him the victory over Goliath. In the same way, kids today can be victorious and do giant things that seem impossible.

Another king in the Bible shows us what can happen when a child is raised to hear God's voice and is obedient to His direction. Josiah was only 8 years old when his father, the king, was murdered. The people chose Josiah for their next king. II Chronicles 34 tells us very little about his early life, but it mentions his mother's name. I believe his mother took a look at this child's future and began pouring into him, explaining and teaching him the ways of the Lord. The Word says, "He did right in the sight of the Lord, and walked in all the way of his father David, nor did he turn aside to the right or to the left." (2 Kings 22:2 NAS) What a legacy!

He reigned righteously for 31 years. The people had fallen away from God, but somehow, Josiah felt the need to call them back. I believe his mother, and perhaps others around him, helped to encourage, teach, guide, and pray over this little king. They worked on their "arrow"- polishing, grinding, and straightening until the day came when God pulled him out of His quiver and said, "NOW it's time".

When he was 16, Josiah began to get serious about God and started the repair of the temple, which had fallen into neglect over the years. The high priest found the Book of the Law, which had been forgotten and lost in the temple. He brought this to Josiah, and when the king heard the law being read to him, the Bible says he tore his clothing and immediately repented for the people's sin and turning from God.

This began his march to bring the people back to the ways of their fathers and to restore Godly worship once more in the land. He tore down all the idols that were in the temple and in the city. Josiah put to death all the idolatrous priests and demolished the altars and even the utensils of the wicked high places. He even went so far as to have the bones of the dead priests dug up, brought to the fire, and burned. This kid was serious!

Josiah then made a covenant with God before the people and said they were now to follow after and worship only the God of their fathers. Over the next years, Josiah did what God called him to do, restoring true worship and repairing the relationship of God and man. He went on to become one of the most righteous kings in the Bible. All because someone took the time to feed this child – to see what he COULD become and to help direct and mold him for the purposes of the Kingdom.

As we pray for our children, let's keep asking God for insight into their lives, for His plans for them, and for how we can give them the tools they need to be prepared for God's assignments. Let's speak over them their destinies. Who knows, we could be raising another David or Josiah! Kids that listen to God's heart, and are used by God for great things!

KIDS CAN GO!

Because, as discussed previously, God is no respecter of persons (Acts 10:34), when children receive Jesus, they get the same whole "benefits" package from God as adults receive. They can "heal the sick, raise the dead, cleanse the lepers, cast out devils" (Matt 10:8). Children can go and "do the stuff", sometimes more effectively than adults, due to their level of innocence and purity. Kids can hear from God, and learn to be obedient at a young age. God can give them anointing just as He does adults, and they can also receive power from Him. The verse, "I can do all things through Him who strengthens me" (Phil 4:13 – NASB), applies not only to adults; it also applies to children whom God loves and calls to be strong leaders.

Because we are to raise our kids "in the way they should go" (Prov 22:6), it seems to me that missions ought to be included. Jesus said in Matthew 28:19, "Go therefore and make disciples of all the nations" (NASB). I do not see in any translation where He indicated that this was an "adults only" club. We are ALL to go. It is a command. Therefore, we are also responsible for training the children under our care to do the very same thing – go.

This does not mean that children should all become full-time missionaries; although, God may call a very select few to that position, and, if so, it will be obvious to all. I do believe, however, that part of their training should include some form of short-term mission work, because the experience and focus helps to sharpen their walk with the Lord and broadens the scope of their world vision.

There are numerous activities that children could participate in at their church that would give them a taste of the type of experience a full-on mission trip affords. Their training could include serving others during select local activities such as a food drive, giving out Christmas baskets to the needy, or assisting in a neighborhood Vacation Bible School outreach. It could broaden to citywide outreaches, especially where other children are the focus, or participate in ministries such as handing out water bottles and food to the homeless in the summer.

There are many opportunities for kids to go and minister, and the more they go, the easier it gets for them. It gives them confidence in their own social skills, causing them to gradually become more independent in their thinking, and the Lord blesses them with boldness as their obedience becomes evident. Children's leaders should constantly be looking for activities that would enhance and empower their children's call to missions.

I can recall taking children from our church to the local nursing home on a regular basis to minister there. Just as going outside of the country would be immersing you in a totally different culture, going to the nursing home is a different environment for children who have never been there. In the same way that you would need to learn the culture and be prepared for what you would experience in a foreign country, children need to be taught about where they will be ministering, and to whom. They need to know what they will be walking into and what to expect in the "country" they are going to visit.

We explained to our kids, ages 6-12, that the residents were somebody's grandma or grandpa. In this way, children could identify with the residents better, since most of them had grandparents themselves. There was discussion on how many of them had grandparents, where they lived, what it was like, and how often they saw them. We also talked about how sometimes grandparents live far away from the rest of their family, and they might not get to see their family as much, so it makes them sad. Because of that, our visit would be really special for some of the grandmas and grandpas and they will be blessed to have us there.

Some of our children were concerned over the part about them being sad and that started conversation regarding how we could cheer them up. I told them, "there's nothing softer in the world than a grandma or grandpa's cheek or hand". I challenged them to hold a hand, or give a kiss on the cheek to prove my point! Many, many seniors were blessed that day by children who wanted to see for themselves, and were happily surprised at the results! We talked about the proper way to touch and hug, so we wouldn't "scare them, or hurt them". This was also for protection for the children and to teach prayer etiquette. The children were always so careful to be gentle and the accompanying adults were watchful and observant at all times.

It was necessary to explain to the children about what they might see, smell, hear, or encounter during their visit. Having worked in nursing homes over the years, I knew there would be some things that might appear scary to the kids or cause them to have questions. It was better to discuss them in the safety and openness of our classroom before our visit to prepare them and to avoid embarrassment for residents and our children alike.

We explained to the kids that some of the seniors might appear very sick and might not be able to make it to the restroom in time. Several of our children immediately identified with that, and we heard stories of nights they were sick and had "accidents". Again, identifying with the people you'll be ministering to is so important to children. We never encountered an "ick" or "that's gross". We discussed how some medicines might make the grandmas and grandpas very sleepy. Most children can recall times when they've seen or experienced that for themselves. Understanding breeds compassion.

Before going to the nursing home we told the children that most of the grandmas and grandpas would be so excited to see us that it might be nice to leave something with them so they would remember our visit. We had all the kids make up 3-4 homemade greeting cards and made sure their names were included. It was just a matter of folding construction paper of different colors, and using their creativity to color, sticker, marker and glue sequins to the various cards. They were required to leave some sort of message on the inside, along with their name, and all four sides were to be filled. Sometimes there were more cards than residents, so some seniors were "richly blessed".

There were prepared songs with hand motions and dancing to fill our trip, and afterwards, the kids handed out plenty of cards and hugs. Pictures of those days are still very precious to me. I still see some of those children today as compassionate, loving adults, and many of them on the mission field! What a joy all around!

There are probably opportunities near your town or area that would be beneficial for children to minister in. Just a short drive from our home area is one of the poorest counties in the country. One of our local churches regularly takes food, clothing, and medical supplies there to assist and they minister God's love during a scheduled service time at a local meeting hall. This is a great chance for the kids to meet with and minister love to another person in need, along with helping set up and clean up after an event. Giving these children responsibilities and helping them achieve those goals can assist in teaching them more about what Christ did and what He calls them to do as they walk with Him.

Early in our ministry, God began challenging Sarah, our children's pastor, and I with questions. What is the difference between kids and adults in the Kingdom of God? Can we overcome our own cultural hang-ups about kids and include them in missions? Can children really "do the stuff" like adults when it comes to ministry? Where and when can they go, if at all, and how young is too young? Who should go on mission trips, and why? Sarah and I spent countless hours in prayer, week after week, month after month, asking God to open our eyes and reveal HIS plan to us for what we were being shown. He did not disappoint!

Sarah and I had been praying for opportunities to minister outside of the church. We had seen several groups arise within our kids ministry, such as our dance team, flag team, kids band, drama group, intercessor group, and others. They had all ministered within our church and once in a while outside the church. God then started showing us something bigger. We began sensing a call to take our kids on a regular mission trip outside the state.

The thought alone was enough to scare us, especially since there were no books or manuals on how to do it. We wondered, "How would that look? Who would go, and where would we go?" Again, it was back to prayer time for Sarah and myself. We looked at the scriptural qualifications of children in ministry, and brought the mission slant to it. Again, according to Scripture, we found nothing that prohibited kids from going out. As a matter of fact, if we believed what God had shown us, that children CAN be used and God empowers them, then it just made sense that this would be the next step.

sometimes telling him things they believed they heard from God, until the man was flat out on the floor and still, the boys kept praying. Within another half an hour, all the boys gradually wandered off, except for Sam.

For as long as I live, I will always remember what happened next. Sam kept on praying for the man who was still on the floor and sobbing. Sam stayed next to him for almost two hours with his little hands on the man. As Sarah and I watched, tears began to fall down his cheeks as he silently prayed for this man he did not know. It was obvious that he was in deep intercession for the first time in his life. The tears dripped off his cheeks onto the floor and onto the back of this gentleman who was receiving God's grace, forgiveness and healing.

That, in my opinion, was where Sam crossed the line into God's destiny for him. He entered into that realm where Jesus and he were communing, and compassion and understanding were being poured into his young life. To this day, I still weep at the remembrance of that moment. What a holy time! When they were finished, the man just held Sam for a long time and was totally changed. We didn't get the whole story, but as I remember, the boys prayed things over him that caused him to repent and be healed from several issues all at once. We were so proud of all our kids, but Sam had won his prize for the day, which was the personal presence and anointing of Jesus!

From that day forward he was a changed young man. We never again had the issues with him that we had before that first trip. There were isolated times of correction, but not at ALL like before. What a joy he became over the years! Sam was so willing and ready to help with anything, and he became such a blessing to both Sarah and myself. As we were driving home from the trip, God spoke to me and said, "That is why you take even the hard ones – they belong to ME". Wow! I do not question Him on who to take anymore.

There have been other trips - to Florida, Chicago, Washington DC, Atlanta, and places in between. Everywhere we've gone we have seen the same results with the children – changed lives in kids AND adults. When the children start to receive the anointing of God as they minister, it moves them, and it rearranges their thought processes. There is a boldness and a confidence which we have seen come over these little warriors that is amazing. They pray over people with such power, and they go after the devil when they feel the need to!

We have had comments from the recipients after the children minister like, "How did they know what I've been asking God for?" and "I never felt so much power in my life come from prayer like this kid just prayed for me" and "How did you teach them these things?" Sarah and I would just look at each other, laugh and say, "We did nothing – God did it all!" These adults are the ones who can testify about God's anointing on the kids, and how THEIR opinions on children changed dramatically in one encounter!

We always allowed children, ages 8 years old and older, to go on our trips without their parents, but under that age needed parental participation. That always has seemed to work well. On occasion, a few parents of the older children would go. We appreciated their attendance, but they were not always allowed to minister during our programs. God had been very adamant with us that the children were to minister - not the adults. On occasion, however, He moved on us to include the adults in one or two sections, but the children were always the ones who prayed over the adults at the end.

We did have parents watching over the children, praying over the kids as they ministered. We also had the adults serve as sounding boards during the ministry time. If a child felt led to give a word to an adult, they would run it by one of our parents to check. This served several purposes. The adult was able to validate the word the child heard, instructed them on how to say it - how to minister the word - and to encourage the child. Then, the parent would stand behind that child as they delivered the word, holding them up in prayer, and directing them if needed. Above all, the children were the ones ministering with an adult backing them up.

It was amazing to watch the parents of these children react to their kid's participation. Some parents wondered why these kids could do all their chores on the trip with no complaining but couldn't pick up the clothes off their bedroom floor at home! Others were surprised their kids knew so much Scripture, or could speak so boldly in front of a room full of strangers. We also had those moms and dads who openly wept in front of us as they saw their little ones powerfully minister God's healing, salvation and restoration. Oh, that we would pour into our kids as they walk beside us, not behind us.

Every trip we'd go on, we tried to have one day off and do something fun just for the kids to relax and be rewarded for their hard work. On one occasion, we took them to stay in a hotel for one night on our way home. You would have thought we had just made them millionaires! As we were unpacking the vans into hotel rooms, I was busy with arrangements and didn't see the mass exodus of kids out to the parking lot. Upon checking it out, I found all of them, along with the adults, praying over a man in the parking lot.

The man had an inoperable brain tumor and had been in major pain from headaches for the last 3 years or so. The pain was constant - every day, every minute. He awoke with it each morning and went to bed with it each evening. He told us there was nothing the doctors could do, and the medicine they gave him for the headaches was practically useless. Eventually, he was told, this would incapacitate him totally and he would die.

Our kids, being taught that nothing is impossible with God, and to have BIG faith, automatically began to lay hands on and intercede for him. Several minutes later, he began shouting, "It's gone! It's gone!" His pain had left completely! He was shouting, which was something you do not do with a major headache. He was dancing around the parking lot and told the kids that the pain in his head was gone after all these years. It was amazing; the kids cheered and rejoiced with him, and then went back to unpacking. It was second nature to them to see miracles – to expect God to do what they asked for and believed in.

As I went up to the front desk to finish checking in, this man came bounding into the room, all smiles, and proceeded to tell everyone there that these kids prayed for him and he was healed – no headache! It was so much fun to watch. He didn't know I was with the kids, so it was even better when I stated that God must love him to heal him in that way. He readily agreed and went on telling people, "You don't understand – I've been in pain for over 3 years and now it's gone!" Isn't God awesome?

The next morning, as we were packing up to leave, our newly healed friend came barreling out of his first floor room, slapping the kids on their backs and hugging them. He told us that this was the first time in years that he had awakened with no headache. He just could not believe it! The kids were quick to tell him that God had healed him because of His great love for him. God was so proud of those bold, anointed warriors that day, and so was I.

We regularly taught the children that God's Word is REAL and alive. If God said it, it is true and not a lie. Therefore, if God tells us we can heal with a word, then we can do it. If God tells us to cast out devils, then we can do it. Our kids became the coolest intercessors ever. Their faith was pure and they wanted to see results, which they did. When we shared with them how they could hear God's voice and that He would tell them secrets about people (words of knowledge -I Corinthians 12:8), they were really excited and wanted to practice constantly. There were times on the trips when we would stop at a public place, such as a mall or a park, and allow them the opportunity to minister.

Once at a park, we gathered the kids and told them that we were going on a prayer scavenger hunt. They broke into groups of three or four and, along with an adult, were given a list of people to pray for before getting back onto the bus. The list contained descriptions like: someone wearing glasses, a little kid, someone with a cane or walker, any person with a book or newspaper, an old person, etc. It was a big park, and there were lots of people out on that beautiful day. Our kids were taught to first greet the person and then to tell them what they were doing. Next, they were to ask if there was anything they could pray for them about that day. It was a very rare occurrence when someone didn't allow them to pray.

Think about it. If a little child came up to you and asked sweetly, "Can I pray for you", what would YOUR reaction be? There is something so pure about a child. Their innocence and purity are the things that make them strong. God just attaches Himself to that purity, and to every effort put forth by children. Most adults do not expect what they get in return when a young prayer warrior gets hold of them! It is almost like a "sneaky maneuver" on the part of the Lord to send out little secret agents disguised in children's skin! The enemy doesn't see them coming.

After getting permission to pray for them, and permission to lay hands on their shoulders, arms, or hands, they began praying with fervor! The parents reported that most people kept their eyes shut, but some were so overwhelmed by the prayers that they opened their eyes to watch what the kids were doing. Our parents received lots of comments about the politeness and the zeal of the kids, and on the power. "I've never heard anyone pray like that, especially a kid," was a frequent response. Many people were moved to tears by the prayers and the simplistic message of God's love from an 8 year old boy or girl, right there in the middle of the park.

Of course, that one person who was fortunate enough to be the only one in the park with glasses got ALL the kids wanting to pray for him! Once the children checked off the items on their list (and had lots of practice ministering in prayer), they ran back to the van and told us about how they prayed with the mayor of the city, or a man with cancer, or a mom who cried when they prayed. It was amazing! Every single one of them wanted to go out and pray for more people. It is safe to say that our kids were addicted to prayer.

On our trips we had the kids doing skits, singing, doing some flags or dances, maybe giving testimonies, leading worship with our kids band, and, once in a while we had a child give a brief message about a certain topic. They were not professionals; they were children. God gave them the boldness; we just provided the transportation and guidance.

There were some programs at churches for the entire congregation and some just for the children. We also did programs at half way homes, shelters, private ministry settings, and hospitals. There were plenty of public ministry times in malls, on the streets, in parks, and at gatherings. We even went to homeless shelters and ministered to the homeless who were sleeping on the street or on park benches. Everywhere we went, God showed up and lives were changed, touched, or encouraged. He was leading the way, and we were just along for the ride. Those kids never really needed Sarah and I – except that they just don't give driver's licenses to children!

There are many more stories of what God did with kids who were empowered, encouraged and equipped - like the story of the man at the amusement park we visited on our day off. We were all on a shuttle, ready to go on a tour, when there was a commotion on the sidewalk outside. A man had fallen to the ground, and his wife was holding him while screaming for help. As we watched, right outside our window, someone checked his vitals and said that he was not breathing and did not have a pulse. I believe his tearful wife was telling people he had a bad heart.

Our kids immediately looked at Sarah and I. Those children knew what to do before we even had a thought. Everyone ran off the shuttle and asked if we could pray for him. Those kids began to intercede for this man, and laid hands on him. As the moments ticked by and we heard sirens in the distance, the man began to cough and move, and then he sat upright! The emergency medical technicians were soon there, and his wife could only thank us as they took her bewildered, but very much alive, husband to be checked out.

Wherever the Lord took these kids, He always had a plan and He always showed up in one way or another. If the people didn't get ministered to or grow, the children did. It was always a win-win situation for God. Seeds were planted, harvests were reaped, and God got the glory everywhere we went.

Even in different cultures, missions are an awesome opportunity to learn how to reach out to children and adults alike with God's love, power, teaching and healing. The experience changes lives, both theirs and yours, and it realigns God's vision in your heart. It reconstructs your worldview as you see God work in a multitude of ways. I, personally, have been humbled and filled with awe at God's diversity as I have ministered in many places.

My first personal mission trip was to Mexico with John and Shirley Tasch of Tasch Ministries, International. They have, for years, introduced children and young teens to the mission field, empowering and encouraging them that they can win people for Jesus anywhere. Their hearts are to set young people on fire for Him, and they facilitate that through service and ministry all over the world. That first trip sold me. I have now traveled to many other countries, and I love ministering to both kids and adults.

I learned so much on that first trip; my eyes were opened, not only to the situations encountered in Mexico, but to what Jesus was beginning to say to me about my own life and where I was headed. "What did I really believe about the Great Commission? Did Jesus' plan for me actually include ministering outside of my own city, state, or country?" The answer was a resounding, "YES"!

Sarah and I took a couple of girls from our children's ministry along with us on that first mission trip and we saw their lives transform before us. We saw pride being crushed as they slept on floors, bathed in a sink, and knelt in the dust to pull weeds. There was compassion being birthed in their hearts as they held little children dressed in soiled clothing who clung to them, or gave out rice and beans to a single mom almost as young as they were. These girls learned to pray over the sick, give their testimony in public, and lead people to Christ without shame or holding back. When we returned, their lives were forever changed and we realized that God had made His mark on them.

As you have read this chapter, you may still be asking, "Can children really go on international mission trips?" Yes they can, and should. I have been on trips outside the country with kids and I have seen over and over again the power of God in transforming their lives, their vision, and their hearts. When trips are done with His heart, His direction and guidance, and in His timing, He can pour into these little warriors in ways we cannot fathom. The confidence, empowerment, maturity and faith that comes from children reaching out to others through missions is undeniably attainable and certain.

Let me ask you a question, "What's stopping our children from being more like Jesus this very day?" I do not mean things like being obedient, kinder, or nicer to their siblings. I mean things like healing the sick, raising the dead, and proclaiming His name to thousands - with power! Do not tell me it can not be done because I have already seen it in action. Equipping the children to hear God's voice, teaching them to have a relationship with Him, then taking them to the streets to practice it is just what Jesus did with His disciples.

I believe there is a time coming when there will be so many people coming to Jesus on a consistent basis, that we will not have time or energy to minister to everyone. Why can we not begin now to train up, prepare, and pour into our children, who will then be able to minister by our side during that time? We need to be asking God for direction, for opportunities, for wisdom, and for clarity in what we should be doing to encourage and build them up. Remember, this is not my idea, it is God's; He is waiting for you to ask Him.

Missions are a great way, in a short time span, to teach, train, and allow a platform for your kids to experience the power and faithfulness of the Lord. Start in a small way by allowing them time to pray over those in your church where it is safe for them to begin praying for others. Then, with training and with God's leading, gradually take them out to different venues and watch what happens! Remember the Great Commission? Not only should we all take His Gospel to the ends of the earth but, because of His love, kids can go too!

KIDS CAN SPEAK!

There are stories that would continue forever in order to tell of the mighty exploits of children who have been filled with the Holy Spirit, recognized their place in the Kingdom, been fueled by their deep love for Jesus, and become on fire for more of Him. I have seen first hand how children can be touched by God and thereby marked for eternity. There are countless tales which relate the amazing things that children have heard and seen, miracles accomplished after prayer, and lives that have been changed, as these little warriors impart to others and move by God's direction.

Many children have experienced God's infilling, understanding and power; we cannot possibly record every story here. Many more children are receiving now, all around the world, even as you are reading this. God is faithful, and He wants to move on His children in deep ways – ALL His children!

This chapter contains comments from just a few of the many children and adults who have experienced God's touch in their lives. All of these testimonies are from kids and parents who have participated in mission trips, gone to camps, received training, and been part of our children's ministry in different churches. Lots of these children are now sharing what God has done in their lives with others. They are moving toward leadership positions in the marketplace, in ministry, in missions, in music, and in life!

As you read their comments, be encouraged, knowing that these could be the children in YOUR family, ministry or church. They are all different ages, from all different types of families and situations, but they all have a common focal point; they love Jesus and have been empowered to share Him with the world! Your children can also have the same impartation. God can move on any child at any time.

These testimonies are straight from the children, with very little changes made in grammar or delivery. Enjoy their pure, simple hearts, and catch their vision as they share with you what God has done in them and through them! Our prayer is that you will become encouraged and motivated to bring Jesus deeper into the lives of those children you are with.

As a child, being on those mission trips, I was filled with a sense of amazement as I watched God work through me. Being able to participate in God's kingdom here on earth by ministering and praying for His Body has impacted the way I live ten years later. If I carried anything away from our trips, it would be 1Timothy 4:12. "Don't let anyone look down on you because you are young. But set an example for the believers in your words, faith, love, and purity." – EMILY

Missions has always been a huge part of my life, but it wasn't until recently when I realized how they all played a part in the plan God has for me. In the children's ministry at our church, we would go all over the place telling people the good news of Jesus Christ. In the summer of 2009, I went to a children's home called "His House" for kids who had been taken away from their parents, orphaned, or thrown over the border in hopes for a better life. I worked with 4-7 year olds and absolutely fell in love with their sweet spirits and loving nature. God started speaking to me immediately and I knew my future would hold more of these moments with children exactly like them. I went back the following year, in the summer of 2010, but this time got placed with the teenagers. I was a little nervous at first due to the fact that they wanted nothing to do with us. I was asked if I would like to switch groups but I knew God had placed me here for a reason, so I rejected the offer. As the week went on God started opening their hearts and they began to accept our love and gave us even more in return. They began to tell me their stories and how their life had changed after coming to "His House". The brokenness was obvious, but it was also obvious that God was doing immense work in their lives. God used this week and the previous summer's week to show me both sides of the life they have: the free spirited one, and the hard one that they try so hard not to show. The day came to leave and, of course, I was an emotional wreck not wanting to go. Within the next few weeks I was faced with the decisions for college: where to go, what to major in, etc. One night I was having a dream about "His House" and in that dream I was an adult, loving on the kids and working with the kids. God woke me up in the middle of it and I felt him say, "This is exactly what you're supposed to do." I will be graduating in the spring and going straight into college to pursue a degree in Social Work. I will eventually apply for a job at "His House", in Miami, Florida and when the time is right, God will open the doors necessary to fulfill His plan. – BETHANY

My first experience on the mission field was when I was 7 years old. It has changed my life to see the need of others instead of my own. I realized how blessed I am to have a family who loves God and people. I learned a lot about people. I am 17 now, and I still go on mission trips and I have the privilege not only to teach others in many different countries but I also learn so much from the people I come in contact with. - ELI

I can say that the kids worship team was the platform that launched me off into later desiring to give God all of my talents for His church's use and His kingdom's expansion. It was my first experience learning to play with a group (on the worship team) and not only that but also learning to worship together while playing. I remember the bonding that took place between my friends and I on the trip. I remember praying for the sick, our worship team playing in various locations, ministering to people in the mall, our drama team performing skits in the different locations, etc.

I have to be honest and say that it wasn't until a couple of years ago that I began to be thankful for the foundation that was built into me by our leaders in those years. As I look at what He has me doing now and as I see the things that He has birthed in me, I am so thankful for the things that they labored to instill in us all. Though it wasn't the fancy sermons or exciting mission trips or the intense games that they came up with - it was simply their example, which is the most underrated ministry tool! I see and know now that their passion for His children wasn't because of the traits in their personalities, it was literally Jesus living through them (Gal. 2:20, 2 Cor. 5:14-15). - JHASON

The mission trips were very powerful! Even as a young girl, I still was very impacted! Not only was the experience of travelling wonderful, but it really gave me more of a gracious heart towards people. It's made me such a grateful woman today and I've learned that helping people is one of the most beautiful gifts of all! I discovered the high of serving others through these mission trips. I will never forget my wonderful leaders and how much they inspired me! They taught me how to love and serve God! Today, I remain to serve others through voluntary work. I will forever be impacted and I am so grateful to have gotten to experience what I did! - SARAH

I believe that participating in mission trips is a vital part of our Christianity. Jesus tells us to go! As a young person in elementary school I went on my first mission trip. This experience shaped who I am. I was at such an impressionable age, and I am so honored to be able to serve God so early. Going on my first trip to Chicago opened my eyes to a new world. Even though the trip was in the United States, I still saw things that I never saw in Tennessee. I remember writing in my journal and saying that I was shocked at seeing all the homeless people on the streets. Growing up in a children's ministry that was so real and with an outreach focus plays a huge part in my life today. To this day I know that I am called to lay my life down to serve others and to serve God. I am so thankful for the encouragement our leaders had in my life. I believe that the only way our Christian young people will not fall into the complacency of typical American Christianity is to open up their eyes to the world around them and to be Christ focused in every area of their life FROM THE START! - KELSEY

Some of my earliest memories of experiencing God's power were on my first mission trip, the Southeast Mission Trip, where we went to the southeast states (Alabama, Florida, and Georgia). Looking back, I know I was supposed to go, and that Satan was trying everything in his power to prevent that. On Monday, four days before we were supposed to leave, my mom came down with pneumonia, and on Tuesday I became very sick, followed by my brother Bradley the next day, and then by my brother Austin on the next. The only person that wasn't going in my family was my dad, and he was the only one that didn't even feel the slightest bit of nausea. By the time Friday rolled around, I was the only one well enough to leave with everyone. Bradley followed the next day, and my mother, and Austin flew in a day or so later. I had several experiences that were quite miraculous to me. At our second stop in Pensacola, FL, at the New Hope House, which was a home for men who had drug and alcohol dependencies, we did skits, dances, and ministered to them. I remember that they got a limited amount of five minute smoke breaks throughout the day and while we were there, they didn't even want to take them. The way that God moved and took precedence over their habits was completely incredible to me. While we were in underground Atlanta, several of us stood in line to pray for a tarot card reader. At first she didn't want us to pray for her because she said that it would disturb her atmosphere. We told her that we just wanted to bless her and then she let us lay hands on her and pray; that was simply incredible to me. This trip gave me just a taste of how great God is, and it has become more and more apparent to me over the years as God has revealed himself to me. The times of where I had to practice listening to him and really focus on his voice has played such a major part of my life today. It helps me trust in Him to know that I'm taken care of, and my life plan will be revealed to me in perfect timing, all i have to do is listen and wait patiently. - KAYLA

Karen – The home Kayla mentioned was pivotal in several of our children's lives, as well as the men residing there at the time. The men there were originally not very happy to have to go to this "meeting". The director, who had set up the date, warned us that these gentlemen were going through treatment for drug and alcohol dependencies and were going to be offered a smoke break towards the end of our time there. He explained they would probably just get up and walk out of the meeting, so we were to prepare the kids for that. We explained all to the children, but they prayed that Jesus would keep them there so they could hear the gospel and be ministered to. Such faith!

As the smoke break time grew nearer, things were going well, but we worried that the children might be disappointed if all the men just got up and walked out. When time came, not a single man left. Everyone was glued to their chair, and the director was incredulous. He told us later, that had never happened in all his time there! Not only did the men stay, but each man was hugely impacted by what the children delivered, and many of them were in tears, repenting and being healed by God's gracious and forgiving love for them. The children, being directed by the Holy Spirit, covered them in love, hugging and praying for them during the ministry time at the end. Oh, the power of simplicity delivered by purity!

I was reading through my journal from when I was fourteen and came across a section of pages that were written when I went on my first mission trip. One of my favorite memories that I uncovered again from there was when we went to the hospital to pray for a miracle. A small girl had fallen into a neighbor's pool, resulting in the girl being left in a coma. The time we spent with her touched my heart unlike any time before. This was true intercession. The faith that was held by the other kids around me, even younger than me was astounding. We believed and had faith, the Holy Spirit only increasing it as we prayed. I wrote, "Today we got to pray for Cassia. She is such a beautiful little girl. I truly believe she will come out of that coma. She moved her hands and feet as we prayed and she's only done that once before. I started crying the minute I entered her room, the Spirit was so strong. Not only have we impacted the atmosphere on this trip, but the Holy Spirit has impacted us and I can't wait for it to happen again. To think, I used to be called shy and withdrawn! Now I am a very bold lion. I can't wait." – ASHLEY

Karen – This next testimonial is from a young man who moved here to the States from Japan with his family. They were precious, but it was real obvious that he was NOT happy with church, and believed that God was not real in the sense of helping, loving, and being there for us. During one of our kids' camps he attended, I was sure he would be going home after the first night. He made it very clear he would not participate, and tuned us all out. When he finally had an encounter with Jesus, it was very apparent why the enemy had worked so hard to keep him away. Today he has such an anointing on him for revolution, evangelism, and fervor for God. The family has recently moved back to Japan due to work, but I know we'll hear more about this young man as he continues to experience God's love and fire, and impact that nation!

I came to America when I was twelve because of my dad's job. I really hated to come over to America. I had to leave my friends, my church, everything. I was so upset that I decided that I would not talk to anybody as much as possible (wonder where that came from). I went to the church which Mrs. Karen went. I thought church was boring as a grave; I played my Nintendo DS the whole time. That summer was when I went to the camp which she organized. Okay....I really, really, really did not want to go to the camp. BUT, my parents already paid the camp fee, so I had to go. I did not want to waste any money. I think it was the second day of the camp. I was in a really good mood. I had actually made a relationship with the friends there (probably the friends made the relationship with me but...)! That night we had a soaking time. I had had time like this many times before, but there was no time in my life that my heart was as tangible as this. I opened my heart towards Him. God, who had always loved me first, was there. That was something I never knew. I wondered, if He was not real, well, it was as I always "knew" before. But if He is..... Please come in.... He really touched me that night, and I realized that He is real. I got to know the solid rock which I could go to when I was down, and that was how I came back to Him the next year again at camp. - MASAHIRO

By going as a young man and seeing how rough life has been for the not so lucky, God has shown me where I can help and bless others. Even in times when I don't feel like I'm doing anything right, I know God can use even smiles to move people and use the blankets we give to the cold and homeless to change lives. That's how we can serve an Almighty God, and know He wants to use us to serve because without Him those things would mean nothing. - CALEB

The experience of going on a mission trip to Ensenada, Mexico definitely impacted me as a young girl. I was only nine years old and I went with a children's ministry group, without my parents. At first my parents thought I was crazy, but they decided to let me go because I knew I was supposed to. We distributed food and medicine, prayed for people, and spent time working at an orphanage. This helped me realize how fortunate I was in my own life. The whole experience and others developed a desire within me to help alleviate suffering in our world. It gave me perspective about what is important and strengthened my faith. Today all the media messages about needing to constantly improve our appearance or have all these material objects to make us happy are shaping children's lives at a very vulnerable time. Experiences like these, where children may find out how others live and offer their time and attention to a good cause, have the ability to shape more compassionate and aware individuals. - RACHEL

Mission trips were truly a life changing experience for me, particularly the Chicago trip. It's like the difference between powerless Christianity and a God who actually moves and works through you. There's a fire to it - a purpose- you know you are absolutely supposed to be there. I remember when I was ten years old. Before the Chicago trip, I was scared to go, so I told myself I didn't want to because you mentioned we would be sleeping in a homeless shelter. Well, God had other plans for me at ten. When we were talking about it in class, I got real hot and started basically freaking out. I'm pretty sure I cried, and everyone felt a power in the room that was there. It was obvious that God wanted me to go and I could feel it with everything in me, and so could everyone else who touched me.

On the mission trip I remember praying for a man for over an hour in tongues saying everything that came to mind to me at the time. I always prayed for fire - there was a passion there. Where I felt the spirit leading, I would push into it and do what I felt he was telling me. Sometimes it seemed like the Spirit was asking me to do something silly, but I was so one hundred percent certain I was supposed to be doing it, and guess what - things would change! Anyways, I learned that when God moves, listen!   CALEB

Well, we were going house to house and we came to this one house and there was a man in there on glucose. The doctor said that he had only two more weeks to live. It was just me and my dad in there so we prayed and I started to feel the Holy Spirit work in the room. At that moment we told the man and the two ladies in the room that he was healed of his cancer and then the man and his wife accepted Christ into their life. - CONNOR

This is my testimony when I went on the mission trip in 2008. I was nine years old at the time. The first stop we made in Virginia, me, Mrs. Tomita, and another girl on the trip saw a vision of crystals. None of us knew what it meant until the next day when a group of people found a tunnel of crystals. In Washington DC , we went to the Capitol building, the Lincoln Memorial, and met this group of people there in their late teens early twenties. In Baltimore, we went to the middle of the street and did a dance routine in front of a random crowd. They were all looking at us. That is my testimony of the mission trip in 2008. - ETHAN

Karen – The miracle that took place through Ethan still amazes me. During our first evening of his first trip out, he received a vision where he saw many crystals, very big, and he kept hearing that they were new. He said they were beautiful and there were a lot of them. Several others in the group heard the word "crystal" or saw a crystal, but not to the detail that this nine year old little worshipper did. He was just amazed at what he saw, but none of us knew what it meant.

The next day, we heard back from his mother, who had not attended the trip that a discovery had been made in New Mexico that day about a "river of crystals" that was sweeping the scientific world. This crystal river contained microbes not known to man, and was over 4 miles long. It had just been discovered. I believe that young man, in being obedient and going on that trip, was being given a window into another realm and was given a gift of vision that evening. He has heard other words from the Lord for people, and continues to move in His power today!

The mission trip I went on with Mrs. Karen was where I got filled with the Holy Spirit. My first word was "courage". I was only twelve years old. I knew it was God because I felt comforting warmth come over my body and I was so relaxed. For the rest of the trip I kept hearing God telling me "courage" as I prayed over people. - KATLYN

There was a lady in Atlanta that I was talking to and prayed for. She gave me a tape of a song that she had written, and told me that she felt like I would do good things for God with it. It for sure helped me step out of my comfort zone, with talking to people about God and how to relate to people. - HANNAH

I went on my first mission trip to Mexico with our church when I was just 12 years old. It rocked my world!!! We fasted and prayed and saw God move in a mighty way! I was able to go on several mission trips with the kids' ministry of our church, including Chicago and Washington, D.C. Our leaders taught us to seek the Lord for ourselves and that we didn't need to be entertained. I learned so much in the children's ministry! We had quiet time with God to listen for His voice. And boy did He speak! God always amazed us because we saw miracles and healings. Our faith grew! I love to tell people that God uses children so much! They just need to be taught to seek after the things of God. I have graduated college and am working for a Christian organization on Capitol Hill. Isn't God good? - SAVANNA

These were only a few of the children that were impacted by getting close to Jesus, hearing His voice, and moving on His direction. They were encouraged, given a platform from which to use the talents and gifting from God, and reaped the benefits of a close, intimate friendship with the Creator of the universe. I am so blessed to know these kids and watch them grow stronger each day in the knowledge of God!

Even though this book is about children and their relationship with the Lord, a few comments from parents regarding their observations seems to be appropriate. These parents have also been on trips, attended camps, and brought their children to our kid's ministry from church. Their hearts have also been touched, as they have witnessed their children learning to come closer to Jesus and hear His voice for themselves.

The parents also watched their kids move in the anointing, pray over people, lead them to Jesus, witness in front of crowds of strangers with no fear – all to boldly bring the light of the gospel into dark places. These parents have been amazed that their own children moved in such power, knowledge, grace, and wisdom beyond their years. It has changed their vision of children's ministry and changed how they see them.

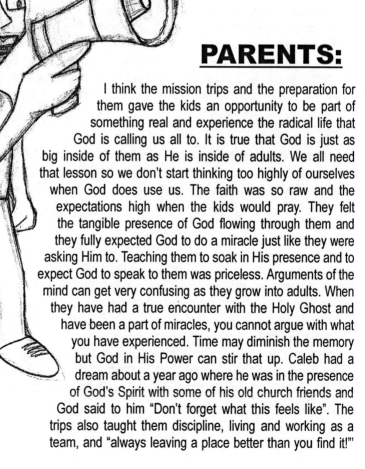

PARENTS:

I think the mission trips and the preparation for them gave the kids an opportunity to be part of something real and experience the radical life that God is calling us all to. It is true that God is just as big inside of them as He is inside of adults. We all need that lesson so we don't start thinking too highly of ourselves when God does use us. The faith was so raw and the expectations high when the kids would pray. They felt the tangible presence of God flowing through them and they fully expected God to do a miracle just like they were asking Him to. Teaching them to soak in His presence and to expect God to speak to them was priceless. Arguments of the mind can get very confusing as they grow into adults. When they have had a true encounter with the Holy Ghost and have been a part of miracles, you cannot argue with what you have experienced. Time may diminish the memory but God in His Power can stir that up. Caleb had a dream about a year ago where he was in the presence of God's Spirit with some of his old church friends and God said to him "Don't forget what this feels like". The trips also taught them discipline, living and working as a team, and "always leaving a place better than you find it!"

Kelsey still wants to be a missionary and is doing missions. Caleb still talks about the woman's leg getting healed after the kids surrounded her in prayer. He still remembers how God shook him to the core with the presence of His spirit when you guys were praying about going to Chicago and Caleb did not want to go but God told him then "YES, I want you to go." I remember that day walking into the children's ministry room and knowing God in His Spirit had been moving and landing and the kids and adults in the room were impacted. - JENNIFER

The day I decided to come to the United States from Brazil as a missionary was the first day of the rest of my life. I have been so blessed to live in this country and be able to share about the love of Christ. I married an American and built my life here. One of my first experiences in the mission field was where I took my son for his first mission trip with the children's team from our church. It changed both of our lives. The bond established on that trip together is still strong today. My son and I went to several mission trips with this church, and I was able to see God move in his life and the people around us. I understand today more than ever how different our lives would have been if we were not constantly reminded about the needs around our world. My mission field has been around my community but I am able to send my son on trips all over the world due to the seed that was planted in his heart when he was only seven years old. I am a blessed mother to have a son that loves God and still have a heart for missions. His experiences started as a seven year old and I pray that will never end. My son started going on his own with other children to share the gospel when he was eleven years old, and today I am forever grateful for those leaders who encouraged us as parents to allow our children to go everywhere and preach the gospel.   - POLLYANNA

I remember going along with the kids from our church on a mission trip to Florida in 2002. We actually took the whole family and made something of a vacation out of it with our children, Wesley, Aaron, Bethany and Matthew, who at the time were about 12, 10, 8 and 6, respectively. It involved some early morning wake-up calls, and we slept on some rather hard floors in sleeping bags, but it was worth the hardship.

The performances the kids did- whether acting out "The Doctor" skit, dancing to "The Hamster Dance", or singing, "I Wanna Be a Lightbulb"- became a platform for the ministry that often happened afterward. The moment that stands out the most for me was when the kids ministered at a homeless men's meeting at one of the churches they were invited to. The men's hearts were disarmed, I think, by the sincerity and innocence that children bring with them, but after the meeting, when the kids asked if they could pray for them, many of them stayed around and let the kids lay hands on them and pray. God was softening their hearts, and I remember my son Wesley, praying for a LONG time over a man. That man was just absolutely sobbing and broken. It made quite an impact on Wesley, and sure made one on me.   - MARK

Bradley got his first guitar for Christmas and we prayed about how to get him lessons. A musician friend heard we got him a guitar and offered to teach Bradley at no charge. What a blessing that was. Bradley learned a lot from Ricky, and went on to teach himself the piano. He writes songs and uses both the piano and guitar! He can hear a song and go to the piano and play it. It is truly amazing!

The trips were always amazing. I was blessed to have been a part of that and witness first hand what God can do through a child as long as they have a willing and receptive heart. I think it is actually easier for children because they don't have the inhibitions that adults have. You tell them something; they believe it and do it! Adults can learn a lot from children!
- AMY

The summer camp and mission trip with Karen....it was impossible for us to forget these precious days, because my sons and I started to see God's glad heart and pleasure. Especially for my first son, Masahiro...God has encountered and touched his whole being through these days. Our leaders always see children as best friends, respect them as though they were adults, train them in His way so uniquely...that makes kids attract to them! During these days Masahiro has totally changed. After the camp I met him, I was able to tell the difference He was changing inside out, yes, it is like overflowing His love, he is no longer dead person(of course in spirit)! I mean his heart was melted by His love and Presence and His people. Karen is so good at hosting Holy Spirit to lead visitation to children. She understands that anybody who has simple heart and faith...especially children can encounter GOD so powerfully. Only in meeting God can people's hearts change sweetly. My three sons have experienced how God is gentle and fun through this camp and trip. They started knowing how exciting thing to show His love and pray for other people passionately. – SUMIYO

There are a couple of things that stand out from the trip we went on. Lana, our daughter, was about nine at the time. When we were having a prayer time with our group one night, all the kids were sitting on the floor of the church where we were staying. It was a group prayer time and various ones were taking part. Lana scooted to the back where I was sitting and sat close to me. I don't remember what the specifics were of the prayers, but Lana began to pray in tongues for the first time. Another thing that stands out was when Bill and I were praying for a teenager at one of the churches where we spent the night. The girl was about seventeen and had scoliosis. We were praying with her about her physical healing and Bill began to pray for her about her future husband. I personally thought he was getting off track, but when he finished the girl began to thank him for that specific prayer. She said that her father was not a Christian and she had been wondering about how she would find a husband when the time came. I am thankful that God is no respecter of age! He will move on anyone who is willing and is seeking Him at any time!

-LESLIE

What an awesome season we walked through with our kids while they participated in the kid's mission program at our church. I think a big lesson that they learned is that the Holy Spirit isn't pint sized in them. The same Holy Spirit that they see move in adults moves also in them! That was proved to them on our mission trips when the kids would lay hands on other children and adults. We witnessed adults falling out in the spirit and weeping as these kids, pure in heart, laid their hands on these people and prayed for them, believing for a mighty move and healing. We watched the kids learn to play instruments, mostly self taught, and put a band together to lead worship. Other kids used their voices and took their worship team on the mission trip. It is amazing to see your children raise their hands to Almighty God in praise and adoration, demonstrating their love and devotion to their Lord and Savior. Our kids are serving the Lord today; one is a worship leader for the teen department at our church, another plays bass, and another plays keyboard when his college schedule and the opportunity present itself. Our oldest, in the military, played drums for a season for a church on his base. God has been so faithful to instill in our children a love for Him and a knowledge and understanding of the power in His name!! - WENDY

These parents were impacted by watching what God was doing through their children. They were grateful to God for the gifting He had placed in them, and then allowed their children to go and "do the stuff". It was just beautiful to watch the moms' and dads' amazement when their child would pray and intercede over adults, and when they gave words of knowledge to them that the children couldn't possibly have known. Watching their kids lead others to the Lord with little effort, and seeing them pray earnestly, with power, brought many parents to tears. They were tears of gratitude for the work God had done in their children's little lives - a work that continues to this day. God is faithful!

Would you like to have the same comments coming from YOUR children and parents? God is doing a NEW THING with our children, and no one is exempt. All are welcomed. Jesus wants to do great things through those who are under your care. Allow Him to move on your children. Give them room to explore His riches and bring them into a place of intimacy with Him. You will be astonished at what God can do!

GROWNUPS CAN!

As you have read this book, hopefully your mindset about children has been challenged. Perhaps you are seeing your child or the children under your care in a new way. That is my prayer. They are a special group of God's unique creations and need to be loved and encouraged as such!

Through our experiences, I hope you have seen how God is not a respecter of persons. Everyone is the same to God, no matter their gender, position in life, or age. Children have the same rights, authority, power, and relationship with Christ as adults have. Kids can do many things. They can go minister with anointing, speak truth and healing into people's lives, hear God's voice with confidence, and be an ambassador for Jesus in the earth. They CAN reach their destiny in Christ.

BUT.......

Kids cannot do this without our help. They need encouragement, training, prayer, mentoring, and someone to walk with them, as their example, to pour into their lives as they learn. They need adults who can envision and understand what God has placed within each child, and then help direct them and feed their calling.

Children need their parents, leaders, and other God-loving grownups to be there with words of praise and pats on the back when they have done well or are working diligently towards their goal. They need people who will get excited about what they have accomplished and acknowledge their growth and obedience. It is important for them to hear those encouraging words little step by little step. That will build them up and give them the faith to press on to accomplish what God has planned for them. When children see adults around them who actually show trust in them, then there is no limit to what they can accomplish!

Kids also need these same people there for them when things have not gone well - to encourage, wipe away tears, speak words to help them stand strong again, and to continue to impact their lives. These young warriors will have their times of testing and failure, just as you and I do. How you help them handle these challenges might make the difference between a confident, excited-for-Jesus child, or a despondent, why-should-I-even-try child. If you can see the call on their life, the promise of God for them, and the destiny they are moving toward, then it is your responsibility to walk that child through the trying times. You can explain to them what is happening, why God wants to use it for their growth and advantage, and how He will do so.

When children make mistakes, they need strong but gracious and forgiving hands and hearts to gently correct and redirect their vision without crushing their spirits or belittling their call. Kids do not need harsh, reactionary comments or anger. What good is that going to accomplish for the Kingdom? They do not need judgmental attitudes or punishments that do not fit the crime. If you will stop for a moment, ask God for guidance, then understand the reasoning behind their behavior, it will shed much light on where the REAL problem lies, and it can be addressed in a Godly manner, for His glory!

Let me encourage you as you finish this book, to examine your own life. In light of this material, have you been challenged about your own belief system, vision or purpose? Have you thought, "I should be doing those things for myself along with my children?" Are there questions in your mind regarding YOUR everyday relationship with the Great Creator?

God is moving with great freedom on those who will give Him their all. That is why I believe we will see more and more children growing in strength, power, and wisdom beyond their years. Children are open, innocent, want to please, and find fulfillment and excitement in serving God. They do not have the baggage to carry that adults have, but they have a purity in spirit that is so refreshing!

The call to motivate, train, encourage and direct your children is not an easy one today, however, as you stay close to Jesus (James 4:8 "Draw near to God, and He will draw near to you"), wait on Him (Psalm 37:7 "Be still before the Lord and wait patiently for Him") and listen for His voice (John 10:27 "My sheep hear my voice, and I know them, and they follow me") you can be assured that God will sustain and empower you. (Deuteronomy 31:6 "He will not leave you or forsake you"). God is FOR you and the children and not against you! He promises to encourage, protect, feed, empower, direct, promote, raise you up, and teach you all things. Jesus loves us, and wants us to have a powerful, exciting and fruitful life – young and old alike.

Jesus said that we need to come to Him as a little child - trusting, without reserve, simplistic, honest, and with a pure heart. He told us in Matthew 5:8, "Blessed are the pure in heart, for they shall see God." Children have that purity, that innocence about them, so they readily hear and see with ease. These are difficult days in the world around us, and sometimes it is a struggle to keep our hearts attentive and attuned to Him. If you ask for His help, He will show you what is necessary to maintain a pure heart and give you the tools to do it.

Take heart, for you CAN do this! If God had not already placed within you the desire to train up your children, you would not be taking the time to read this book! He is looking for willing vessels, available and ready. If you wait upon Him, listen for His voice and be open to new possibilities, you will find strength, wisdom, understanding, creativity, and power. He will show you how to impart that to your children!

The closer your walk with God, the more clearly you will see the call and destiny of those little ones under your care. As you move in intimacy with the Creator of universe, you will hear the secrets about your children that He wants you to know. If you ask Him, God will show you pieces of their future and what nuggets of glory He has placed within them. Then He will give you new thoughts and suggestions for feeding and nurturing those calls.

I would encourage you to stop thinking within the confines of what you HAVE been doing with your children and begin to open your mind to other things that Jesus might suggest. He is a very creative God, and He has some awesome ways of communicating truth! Instead of thinking, "We can't do that", try thinking, "Why CAN'T we do that?" Ask Him for an open mind –that He would open the ears and eyes of your heart and reveal His plans for your children. It might actually be easier and more fun than you would have thought!

It's time for us to stop the "milk and cookies" attitude that has permeated our children's ministries for years and years. We are losing our kids to a huge lie of the enemy that our kids cannot understand or really focus. What if we immerse them in understanding what the words to the worship songs sung on Sunday morning mean? What if we allow them time to "soak" in God's presence for increasing amounts of time, just to see what happens? Is anything lost? What do we have to gain? Glorified, Spirit-filled, excited children that are ready to take on any task for Jesus!

What if you take your children out to a nursing home once a month to sing and make cards for the residents? What would this activity build in their little lives? It would help them learn to care for others, to reach out, to minister, and to get rid of selfish attitudes with a focus on others. When you see the smiling faces of the elderly grandmas and grandpas, and you hear the happy, excited pleas of the children to "do this again", will that be payment enough for the "trouble" and time you spend organizing and doing it?

Or what if you had your children hand out water bottles or sandwiches and teach them to pray for the homeless in or near your city? How much is an afternoon of grateful looks, maybe a few tears, and bringing joy to someone who has no one to care for them worth to you and your ministry? What eternal significance will it have upon your children? Will it teach them a broader view of the world around them? Could it teach them about gratefulness for what they have and how to minister to others by taking their eyes off themselves? Will it teach them about our responsibility as Christians to do what Jesus calls us to do?

Imagine if your kids "adopted" a low income or special needs child for a holiday, and they all earned money to purchase toys, clothing, and treats for them. What if they went a step further and invited several of those children to a party thrown just for them and blessed them with gifts, games and love? What kind of lessons would you be teaching your children? What benefits would they (and you) receive, not to mention the recipients that you would be blessing and encouraging? Is it worth the time and effort?

I have seen these things happen. I have been an eye witness to how these things change a child, impact their life, and motivate them to "do as Jesus did". If we want our children to become more like Jesus, why are we waiting until they are grown? We must begin with a few small steps and reach out to the needs in our community. When we ask for Jesus' help, I'm sure He will be happy to give it to us!

We must put an end to the days of nothing but a story and a coloring page handout on Sunday morning. We must get our kids in action – actually DOING what Jesus commanded us to do. They are NOT too young, and youth is the age to impact them for life. Let us get them grounded in the Word, listening for and hearing His voice, soaking in His presence, experiencing God for themselves, while trusting that God will step in and do what He does best – changing and forging lives for the Kingdom.

May the blessing of the Lord be on you as you walk with and impact these young warriors. These could be the most exciting days of your life as you help fashion little lives for God's use. The amazing miracles you will witness, astounding growth you will see and unwavering faith you will encounter from these children will encourage and build your vision for your ministry and for their lives. Now, as we say to our kids…

Get ready...

Get set...

GO!!!

Clown Ministry and two new friends in housing project.

Local children and adults came out to witness dance, clowns, testimonies, skits, prayer, ags and more during presentation and ministry.

Organized as well as Spirit-led activities made ministry exciting and real for the team as well as the receivers. What was Jesus going to do next?

Worship team members work together to set up equipment and do sound check before each ministry service. Trained by adult mentors, they were always ready to go and were prayed up before ministry time.

Team members understood the importance of what they were ministering. They knew if they allowed God to use them and focused on Him alone, lives would be changed, and they were!

Hundreds of lives were impacted and enriched by kids learning to hear His voice and speak His words of comfort, direction, confirmation and power.

Salvation, healing, and impartation came when people young and old yielded to Jesus and allowed His Spirit to flow from the children.

Team members prayed for adults and children alike, sometimes interceding for more than an hour over one person. When finished praying for one individual, the children would look around for more to pray for. Prayer became a major focus on all our trips.

Children as young as five and six were taught respect for people and God. They grew to love and appreciate people of all ages, races, and status.

Love became a main focus of our nursing home ministry. In teaching the children how to understand those around them, they naturally bloomed into caring, sensitive children who are now caring, sensitive adults accustomed to ministry in many areas.

Adults were amazed at the accuracy, power, authority and wisdom beyond the years of the children who were under the leading of the Holy Spirit.

There was always a sweet, tangible spirit in each room during ministry time. There was no rushing, pushing or manipulating. God always saturated the time with His presence, and both team members and recipients felt and recognized Jesus at work in their hearts.

Ministering in outdoor parks, malls, grocery stores, middle of town, on the street or in a building, the enthusiasm and innocence of the team along with the anointing of God and His timing always brought people ready for ministry whether they knew it or not!

The more the team ministered on a trip, the deeper the Spirit was released into their lives. Many children were changed forever by a short time of teaching and doing hands-on ministry.

Praying for each other on a consistent basis was important both before, during and after each trip. This is one place where the children became a team, working together and covering each other daily.

After a few days, there was no need for major direction during ministry times. The children heard from Jesus, ministered to others, and the adults could only stand by and wonder at the wisdom and authority God gave the kids.

Once kids got a taste of what God could do through them, saw the results from those they prayed over, and felt the anointing on them, there was no stopping them!

The children quickly discovered that covering each other during ministry times was important, and allowed more power, clarity and authority to come through.

Ministry time was also a time for rejoicing in the creativity and fun of being a child of the King. God wants children to be themselves, for in that lies the innocence and purity He so dearly loves and longs for in all of us.

No matter where we went, Jesus aligned us not only with people needing a touch from Him, but with other believers. We always exchanged blessings and impartations as we walked together in ministry.

After a few days, no one was ashamed to stop and pray openly for others. This anointing grew as the trips went on, with the children begging to stop and walk through parks and malls, praying as they went.

Ministering to and praying for the homeless was always the most anointed time during a trip. Not only were lives impacted on the street, but the children walked away with a new compassion and understanding that they carry to this day.

It was an amazing thing to watch children as they ran up to the displaced, handing out bags of food, water and toiletries, then praying for and loving on those whom Jesus loves! Purity and love in action equals a world of blessing.

Working together as a team to minister and cover each other, unity is built with love and power freely flowing from the heart of God.

Young and old, boy or girl, God used and empowered every team member to minister effectively and grow together in Him.

Spirit-led times of ministry on the street drew many who received ministry and marveled at what God can do with kids open to His Spirit.

RESOURCES:

TEACHING:
David and Kathy Walters – Good News Ministries
www.goodnews.netministries.org/goodnews.html

John and Shirley Tasch – Tasch Ministries International
www.taschministries.org/main.html

Mark Virkler – "4 Keys to Hearing God's Voice"
www.cwgministries.org

Mark Harper – Super Church Curriculum and Resources
www.superchurch.com

MUSIC:
Vince Gibson/Anna Ivy –
Journey to the Mountain (instrumental)
www.vincegibsonmusic.com

John Belt – The Portals of Heaven / Another Realm /
Sacred Fire / The Soaking Presence
www.liveinhispresence.com/soaking.htm

Alberto and Kimberly Rivera –
Soaking Music (all instrumentals)
www.rainingpresence.com

ART:
Daniel Wornicov – cover art
www.wornicovart.com

Joshua Moffitt – caricatures/children's sketches
Joshua@fire4thenations.com

ABOUT THE AUTHOR:

Karen has ministered to youth and children for over 30 years, in schools, churches, para church organizations and the community. She majored in elementary education in college, home schooled her two daughters, and has been working with children ever since. She and her husband Allen created Fire For the Nations, a non-profit mission organization in 2006, ministering to children and adults in many different countries, including the US, giving humanitarian aid, organizing ministries, working with street children and orphans, preaching, teaching and evangelizing. Karen is an ordained and licensed minister. She and her husband, Allen, have been married for 33 years and currently live in the Nashville, TN area. They have 2 married daughters, and never tire of their 6 anointed grandchildren.

For more information on Fire For the Nations or booking future events, visit their website at: www.fire4thenations.com or email karen@fire4thenations.com.

CPSIA information can be obtained at www.ICGtesting.com
Printed in the USA
LVOW071203220113

316678LV00003B/8/P